EXAMINING RELIGIONS

Islam

FOUNDATION EDITION

Anne Geldart

Heinemann

Heinemann Educational Publishers
Halley Court, Jordan Hill, Oxford OX2 8EJ
a division of Reed Educational & Professional
Publishing Ltd

OXFORD MELBOURNE AUCKLAND
JOHANNESBURG BLANTYRE GABORONE
IBADAN PORTSMOUTH NH (US) CHICAGO

Heinemann is a registered trademark of Reed Educational
& Professional Publishing Ltd

British Library Cataloguing in Publication Data

ISBN 0 435 30325 2

Designed and produced by Gecko Ltd, Bicester, Oxon
Illustrated by Chris Rothero, Barry Rowe, Gill Bishop
and Gecko Ltd
Cover design by Gecko, Bicester, Oxon
Printed and bound in Spain by Edlevives

Acknowledgements

The publishers would like to thank Anne Pringuer for
reading and advising on the manuscript.

The author would like to thank Sue Walton, Jane Tyler,
Robert Bircher and the rest of the Heinemann team, and
her long-suffering husband for his unfailing support.

The publishers would like to thank the following for
permission to reproduce copyright material.

Muslim News for the articles on pp. 128 and 129; Octagon
Press Ltd for the extract from *The Elephant in the Dark* by
Indries Shah on p. 37.

The publishers would like to thank the following for
permission to reproduce photographs.

Abbas/Magnum Photos pp. 22, 54, 66, 73 (both), 74
(bottom), 77; the J allan Cash Photo Library pp. 6 (top),
110 (bottom), 111 (top right, bottom left and right); Circa
Photo Library p. 58; Donna DeCesare/Format Partners
p. 105; Sally and Richard Greenhill p. 102; Robert Harding
Picture Library pp. 93, 143; The Hutchison Library pp. 6
(bottom), 34, 51, 89 (left), 110 (top), 112 (bottom), 122;
Barry Lewis/Network Photographers p. 85; Dr Jean
Lorre/Science Photo Library p. 28; Mohamed Abu Mustafa
p. 80 (right); Ann and Bury Peerless pp. 111 (top left), 112
(middle); Rex Features Ltd p. 127; Peter Sanders pp. 5, 8,
25 (right), 38, 44, 60, 61, 62, 67, 74 (top), 75, 76, 87, 89
(right), 90, 94, 96, 98 (left), 112 (top left and top right);
Frank Spooner Pictures p. 147; Telegraph Colour Library
p. 98 (right); Topham Picturepoint p. 21; Zefa p. 25 (left),
69, 113; All other photographs were supplied by
Ruqaiyyah Waris Maqsood.

Cover photographs by Peter Sanders.

The publishers have made every effort to trace copyright
holders. However, if any material has been incorrectly
acknowledged, we would be pleased to correct this at the
earliest opportunity.

CONTENTS

1 INTRODUCTION

SUBMISSION

Islam is an Arabic word that means 'submission' or 'obedience'. People who follow Islam are called Muslims. They believe that submission to the will of God is the only way a person can have peace in their heart and mind, and in society.

Muslims believe that God exists and His name was revealed in the **Qur'an** as **Allah**. They learn about the will of God through the Qur'an. The Qur'an is a series of messages or revelations from God given to the Prophet **Muhammad**, over a period of 20 years during the sixth century **CE** (Common Era).

Submission to God is the positive act of bringing your attitudes and behaviour into harmony with God's will. Belief and action are equally important. Muslims believe they must keep the Five Pillars of Islam, which are:

- bearing witness to their faith
- praying five times a day
- giving one-fortieth of savings to the poor
- fasting the 30 days of **Ramadan**
- making the pilgrimage to **Makkah** (see unit 32).

> … this is righteousness – to believe in God and the Day of Judgement, and the **Angels**, and the Book, and the Messengers; to give from your wealth out of the love for God to your family, to orphans, to the needy, to the wayfarer, to those who ask, and for the freeing of slaves; to be steadfast in prayer, and practise regular giving; to fulfil all the promises which you have made;… Such are the people of truth, the God-fearing.
>
> (**surah** 2:177)

TRUE ISLAM

Islam is often misunderstood in the West, due partly to ignorance and partly to bad publicity. People react to media reports about terrorist activities carried out by some groups in the Middle East.

The spirit of Islam is against violence, although Muslims believe in defence of the weak. Islam is a religion that teaches about God's compassion (kindness) and guidance to all people. It is a religion based on mercy, peace, forgiveness, modesty and happiness.

> He is not a believer whose neighbour cannot feel safe from his harm.
>
> (Hadith)

A **Hadith** is a saying of Muhammad.

Islam has over 1000 million followers in the world. About 2 million Muslims live in Britain.

People often confuse 'Muslim' with 'Arab' or 'Asian'. This is a mistake. Islam began in an Arab country, but now there are more non-Arabic than Arab Muslims. Also, fewer than half of Muslims in Britain are Asian.

MAKKAH AND THE KA'BAH

The Prophet Muhammad was born in Makkah in Saudi Arabia. Makkah was famous at that time because it had an ancient temple called the **Ka'bah** or Cube, because of its plain cube shape.

There is a legend that the original Ka'bah was built by **Adam**, the first man, and was the first house of God on earth.

At the time of Muhammad there were over 360 altars, statues and religious objects in the Ka'bah. Some were idols worshipped as gods. Others were thought to be a point of power or the home of a god. Many were strangely shaped meteorites or pieces of rock. There were pyramid shapes that were thought to represent the sun breaking through the clouds and bringing the blessing of the Supreme Force to earth.

Pilgrims at the Ka'bah, Makkah

The most important 'gods' in the Ka'bah were Ilah the 'Strong One', and three goddesses thought to be his daughters. These represented the sun (life force), the planet Venus (purity and love) and Fortune (the decider of fate).

THE QURAISH

Makkah was an important centre for trade. Also, thousands of pilgrims visited Makkah to see and worship the idols in the Ka'bah. The **Quraish** had control of the Ka'bah and the water supply in Makkah. They were the most important tribe living in Makkah. They made a profit out of the traders, and also by selling provisions to the pilgrims.

THE HANIFS

The Quraish became very wealthy from the visitors to Makkah and they were selfish. Many other tribesmen were more honourable. They were unhappy with the greed and corruption that seemed to come with the money. These people were called **hanifs**. They would go to pray alone in the silence of the desert and the mountains.

They believed that there could only be one Supreme Power, who they thought must have

created the universe. This Almighty God, they believed, had sent revelations to such prophets as **Musa** (Moses) and **Isa** (Jesus). This God was a spiritual power who could not have physical sons or daughters. He entered the heart of humans, and was not to be found in rocks and idols.

One very religious and highly respected hanif was **Abd-al-Muttalib**. He often spent an entire month praying in a cave near Makkah.

In 570 CE Abd-al-Muttalib's son, **Abdullah**, died suddenly, leaving his young wife **Aminah** pregnant. The boy who was born became known as Muhammad, the Prophet or Messenger of God.

FOR YOUR FOLDERS

Read surah 2:177. Then write two lists:

1 all the things Muslims are called to believe in

2 the practical duties of Muslims.

FOR DISCUSSION

- Do people *always* become selfish when they are wealthy?

- Why do you think people worshipped stone pillars or statues, or the sun, moon and stars? What did these things represent?

*A **Bedouin** and his camel*

By the glorious light of morning, and by
the stillness of night! Your Lord has
not forsaken you, and He is not angry
with you.
Surely your hereafter will be better for
you than the present, and in the end
God will be kind to you, and you be
satisfied.
Did He not find you an orphan, and give
you a home?
Did He not find you [lost and]
wandering, and showed you the way?
Did He not find you in great need,
and took care of you?
As to you, therefore, do not wrong the
orphans, do not turn away those that
ask your help, but proclaim the
goodness of your Lord.

(surah 93)

LEGENDS

One legend about Muhammad said that
before his birth his mother Aminah heard a
voice that told her the child would be a great
leader. Another legend said that two angels

removed Muhammad's heart and washed it
clean. Then they weighed it against a
thousand other men's hearts. Then they said,
'Let it be. Even if you set the whole
community in the scale, he would still
outweigh it.'

Muhammad himself disapproved of all
untruths. He did not like stories that
suggested he had special powers. The
Prophet Isa (Jesus) was the miracle worker,
not himself. He was only a simple and
devout (devoted to God) man, whom God
had chosen to receive the Qur'an (see surah
7:188, page 13).

EARLY TRAGEDIES

Quraish women used to entrust their babies
to Bedouin women (wandering tribespeople)
who took them to the pure, clean air of the
desert to bring them up. Muhammad lived
with **Halimah** the Bedouin until he was six.

Sadly, his mother died the year he returned
and he became an orphan. At first his
80-year-old grandfather, Abd-al-Muttalib
took him in.

Two years later he also died and Muhammad
went to live with his uncle, **Abu Talib**, a
wealthy merchant.

The Prophet worked as a shepherd

MUHAMMAD GROWS UP

First, Muhammad worked as a shepherd.

Later, his uncle began to take him on business journeys. He earned the nickname *al-Amin*, 'the Trustworthy One'.

MUHAMMAD GETS MARRIED

When he was 25 years old, Muhammad was employed by a wealthy widow called **Khadijah**. She was very impressed with his hard work and fair dealings. He was also young, handsome and devout. Khadijah was 40 years old. She found the courage to ask Muhammad to marry her.

She became his only love and stood by him through all his difficult times until she died 25 years later.

They had six children: two sons, Qasim and Abdullah, and four daughters, Zainab, Ruqaiyyah, Umm Kulthum and **Fatimah**. The two boys died in infancy.

ALI AND ZAID

When Abu Talib was in need, Muhammad repaid his kindness to him by taking in his little son **Ali**.

Zaid ibn Haritha was a slave boy of Khadija. One day Zaid's father discovered where he was and offered to buy him back. Zaid said he would rather stay with Muhammad.

Muhammad was so moved that he freed the boy instantly, and raised him as his own son.

> There are four qualities in a hypocrite:-
> when they are trusted they cheat;
> when they talk, they lie;
> when they give promises, they break them;
> when they argue, they are abusive.
> Those who show the most perfect faith are those who are kindest to their families.
>
> (Hadiths)

TALKING POINTS

- Muhammad's feelings might have been different if he had not suffered himself, and if people had not been kind to him.

- What does surah 93 (opposite) teach about God's feelings towards those in trouble?

THINGS TO DO

Look at the Hadiths (sayings of Muhammad) above. What do they tell us about his teachings about a person's character?

FOR YOUR FOLDERS

1 Explain the parts played in the life of Muhammad by Halimah, Abu Talib and Khadijah.

2 In what ways do you think Muhammad showed he was a 'fine man'?

3 What does this unit tell you about his character?

4 Why do you think Muhammad was worthy to be chosen by God as a prophet?

5 Why did Muhammad disapprove of flattering legends about himself?

Truly, We have revealed this [Message] on the Night of Power...; on that night the angels and the spirit descended by permission of God, and all is peace till the breaking of the dawn.

(surah 97)

THE SPIRITUAL SEARCH

Muhammad often went out to the hills to be alone in order to pray. Sometimes he stayed out all night. He spent his life searching for spiritual guidance, drawing closer to God.

Like most people of his time, he could not read or write (surah 7:157–8 calls him 'unlettered'). Even so, people who knew him respected him as a man close to God, who was thoughtful, kind and wise.

Muhammad knew the Ka'bah and its many shrines and altars. He also knew the greed and corruption of the rich merchants. These men exploited the poor, who prayed hopefully to their idols.

THE REVELATION

One night in the month of Ramadan in 610 CE, when Muhammad was 40 years old, something happened that changed his life. This night became known as the Night of Power, or **Laylat-ul-Qadr**.

Muhammad was alone, praying in a cave on Mount Hira (later named **Mount Nur**, or Hill of Light). Suddenly he heard a voice calling his name and saying '**Iqra!**' ('Proclaim!' or 'Recite!'). He saw a roll of silk with letters of fire on it, but could not read what it said.

The angel **Jibril** who appeared to him was the same angel who appeared to the prophet Ibrahim and to **Maryam** (Mary) the mother of Isa (Jesus). Isa was the founder of the Christian religion. Now Muhammad was also to become God's messenger or Prophet.

Three times the angel ordered Muhammad to read aloud and each time he replied that he could not. He felt so tense, it was as if something had seized his throat so tightly that he was going to die.

Suddenly the Prophet knew in his heart what the words said, and began to recite them.

Mount Hira, where the Prophet received his first revelation

THE MESSAGE

Proclaim! In the name of your Lord and Sustainer who created Man from a clot of congealed blood, speak these words aloud! Your Lord is the Most Generous One –
He who has taught the Pen,
who reveals directly
things from beyond human knowledge.

(surah 96:1–5)

THE WAITING

After this experience the Prophet struggled home to Khadijah, trembling with shock. He was full of doubt. How did he know that he was not being tricked by the devil into trying to claim something about himself that was not true?

He told Khadijah everything. She wrapped him in his thick cloak and helped him to sleep. Khadijah's cousin, **Waraqa ibn Nufal** had become a Christian and had translated the Gospels into Arabic. He was nearly 100 years old and blind, but Khadijah respected his judgement. Waraqa was sure that God had indeed sent His revelation to her husband.

Thus Khadijah became the first to believe the Message he revealed. The next were Ali, then aged ten, and Zaid. Soon, Muhammad's friend **Abu Bakr** also believed. At this stage the Prophet did not talk about his experiences openly.

THE WAIT

Muhammad had no new revelations for two years. This was a test of his faith, and he became anxious about what it might mean. At last the angel came again. The time had come for Muhammad to go out and proclaim the messages he was receiving, in public.

O you, wrapped [in your cloak] – arise and warn! Glorify God! Make your garments pure! Give up all uncleanness. Give, without expecting any return. For the sake of your Lord, endure with patience!

(surah 74:1–7)

FOR DISCUSSION

Muhammad had always been a devout man. In what ways do you think his life was different after the Night of Power from before?

FOR YOUR FOLDERS

1 Imagine you were one of Muhammad's close family. Write about what happened on the Night of Power and explain what convinced you that what the Prophet told you was true.

2 What would have happened if the Prophet had given in to doubt?

3 Explain what the surahs quoted in this unit teach about God and His relationship with the Prophet.

QUICK QUIZ

1 What was the name of the angel?

2 What does the command 'Iqra!' mean?

3 What was the name of Khadijah's Christian cousin?

4 Name the first four Muslims.

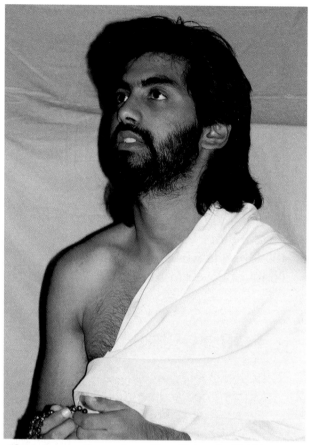

'God chooses those whom He will' (surah 42:13)

The Prophet was not well educated. He was simply a very devout person. God chose to make Himself known to him.

TAQWA – AWARENESS OF GOD

Religious awareness can be a bit like falling in love. You may have been a happy and contented child. Suddenly you meet someone and fall 'head over heels' in love. You feel emotions you never knew before: joy, belonging – and suffering. Your life takes on new meaning, and nothing can ever be the same again. You can't explain this experience to a child who has no awareness of it.

There are other moments of truth in life. For instance, when you realize you are totally alone and no one can help. Only you (and God) can go through this moment – such as childbirth or the discovery that you are going to die. These may be moments of special awareness and afterwards your life is totally changed and you can never go back.

For Muslims, **taqwa**, or awareness of God, is like being 'born again'. New believers see everything in a new light and their life becomes changed for ever.

You can be a good and honourable person without ever having this experience. But when it happens, the most obvious change that comes over you is conviction – belief. For a Muslim, to know God is to submit. To accept Him is to hand over control of life to God's guidance.

> Wait with patience for your Lord's commands; and don't be like the prophet Jonah who cried out in agony. If grace from his Lord had not reached him he would indeed have been cast off on the naked shore, in disgrace. But your Lord chose him, and placed him among the righteous. Unbelievers might well stare at you and call you mad when they hear the Message – but it is nothing less than a Message to all the world.
>
> (surah 68:48–52)

RECEIVING THE MESSAGES

The Qur'an consists of messages given to the Prophet. He told these messages to his friends, who memorized them and wrote them down so that nothing would be lost. Muslims believe that these messages were not just the thoughts and teachings of the Prophet, but the words of God that were sent down to him.

- The special revelations were always accompanied by strange happenings, like shaking or trances.

- The Prophet always knew when they were about to happen.

- Sometimes he lay down and covered himself in his cloak.

- Sometimes he seemed to lose consciousness.

- Sometimes he became very hot and was soaked in sweat, even in cold weather.

- Sometimes the voice was not clear. One tradition claims that he said, 'Sometimes it is revealed like the ringing of a bell… This state passes after I have grasped what is inspired.'

- Sometimes the message came unexpectedly, while he was out riding or being questioned by the public.

- On a few occasions the angel Jibril appeared in the form of a man to give the revelations.

The Prophet's visions always seemed like a near-death experience. He felt he was leaving his body and might not be able to come back to it. Afterwards, he would be back to normal, sit up and repeat what he had been taught.

MUSLIM BELIEFS ABOUT THE QUR'AN

- Muslims believe that God used the Prophet to reveal the words that were written in the Qur'an.

- The Qur'an is not a book *about* the Prophet. However, some revelations came to him to help deal with particular problems he faced.

- Many people did not believe the Prophet. They wanted him to work miracles like the Prophet Isa (Jesus). He replied that the Qur'an itself was the supreme miracle.

- People who did not believe in God said the messages were the product of the Prophet's own mind, and even suggested he was mad or possessed by evil spirits.

Certainly the Prophet's mind and body were 'receiving equipment'. There is no way to prove whether or not the equipment was faulty. We can only examine the messages, and the life and influence of the Prophet.

The Qur'an is clear about these matters.

> You are not mad or possessed, by the grace of your Lord. Your character is above the standard that can be slandered. Soon everyone will see which of you is really mad…Take no notice of despicable slanderers.
>
> (surah 68:2–6,10)

There have been some mad or misguided individuals who have claimed divine revelation. When you study their words and actions, it becomes clear that what they did or said was not 'from God'.

FOR YOUR FOLDERS

1 Make a list of things the Prophet's family and friends saw when he was receiving revelations.

2 What did believers say to those who wanted to see miracles?

3 Explain the difference between 'sent down' revelations and personal inspiration.

FOR DISCUSSION

- How might a person tell whether their belief that they are doing God's will is really true?

- God cannot be seen or proved. Neither can the existence of love. What evidence could you use to 'prove' that love exists?

THE MESSAGE

When Allah ordered the Prophet to go out and preach in public, he went straight away. He had to make people believe that there *was* a True God. They had to realize that there was life after death, and a time of judgement when they would be punished or rewarded for the way they had lived.

The Prophet told them that even if they didn't believe this now, when it actually happened they would want to be forgiven for the wrong things they had done. But it would be too late. Life is a test – and if they failed, they failed.

He said that God was merciful and knew everyone's true motives. If they were truly sorry, He would forgive them. But God was also truly just. If people did bad things while they were alive, and were not truly sorry when they died, then He would not forgive them. That would not be fair, and God was always fair.

The earlier prophets like **Ibrahim** (Abraham), Musa (Moses) and Isa (Jesus) all gave the true message. Now Muhammad also put God's commands to them. People were free to choose. If they refused to listen, then whatever happened was their own fault.

The Prophet taught that a person's first duty was to God. This was more important than links with family or tribe. People had to learn the difference between the True God and idols.

THE REACTION

The people of Makkah were amazed when the Prophet began to preach openly. They knew him as a kind, gentle and wise man – but now he was claiming that he had received messages from God and that he had been sent to change their lives.

Crowds gathered, but they jeered at him. Few wanted to change their selfish ways. When the Prophet's own tribe realized he was trying to stop people worshipping the idols in the Ka'bah, they were furious because they thought they would lose money over it.

They attacked the Prophet with insults, ridicule and threats. When this did not work, they accused him of being a sorcerer. They said he insulted the gods and was trying to split up families by turning young men against their fathers. The Prophet's uncle, a tribal chief, tried arguments, bribery and threats – but nothing would make him give in.

Those who joined the Prophet became known as Muslims. Many were hurt. An Ethiopian slave, **Bilal**, was left to die in the sun with a huge rock on his chest. Abu Bakr rescued him.

The bravery of the Muslims impressed some people, including the Prophet's uncle, Hamza, a famous warrior who joined them. The Prophet's enemies grew more worried when they saw that important people were beginning to believe his message.

> By the star when it sets, your fellow man [Muhammad] is not mistaken, neither has he been misled. He does not speak from mere impulse. The Qur'an is nothing less than inspiration sent down to him. One mighty in power taught him, one full of wisdom.
>
> (surah 53:1–7)

THINGS TO DO

1 Why were the merchants of Makkah so against Muhammad and his message?

2 Why do you think the Prophet's message might have been successful with poor people, women and slaves?

'In His service'

ABU TALIB'S PROTECTION

Abu Talib was the Prophet's protector. Abu Talib's brother, **Abu Lahab** tried to make him disown him. Abu Talib was very upset by the rift growing in his family. He begged the Prophet to give up his mission. He said, 'Spare me and yourself; do not put a greater burden on me than I can bear.' The Prophet answered, 'O my uncle, by Allah, if they put the sun in my right hand and the moon in my left in return for giving up this cause, I would not give it up until Allah grants victory to the Truth, or I die in His service!' Abu Talib, greatly moved, swore he would *always* protect the Prophet.

FOR YOUR FOLDERS

1 'Ridicule (mockery) is an extremely hurtful form of torture, but it can also make you strong if you survive it.' Do you think this is true? How does it apply to the Prophet's experience?

2 It often seems difficult to impress people in your own family. Do you agree? Explain your answer.

THINKING POINT

I have no control over what may be helpful or hurtful to me, but as God wills. Had I the full knowledge of the Unseen, I should increase the good, and evil should not touch me. I am only a warner, and an announcer of good tidings to those who believe.

(surah 7:188)

● The Prophet's critics claimed that if he were a genuine prophet, God would protect him. How does the above passage answer this criticism?

THE YEAR OF SORROW

When the Prophet was 50, ten years after he received his call, his uncle Abu Talib died. Soon after that his beloved Khadijah also died at the age of 64. The Prophet was plunged into deepest sorrow, though he accepted that death must come to all.

His enemies took advantage of his difficulties. They despised and humiliated him. Abu Lahab's wife threw rubbish and thorny branches outside his house every day. (Later, when she was taken ill, the Prophet did housework for her until she recovered.)

REJECTION AT TAIF

Three years before this, some Muslims had moved away to Abyssinia, a Christian country. The Prophet tried to preach in **Taif**, but the people there laughed at him and encouraged youths to throw stones at him. This was the saddest day of his life.

LAYLAT-UL-MI'RAJ

During this time of persecution, the Prophet had a great experience called the Mi'raj. Mi'raj means 'ladder' or 'ascent' and refers to something Muhammad saw on his Night Journey, or **Laylat-ul-Mi'raj**.

The Qur'an does not say much about this event, but states only that glory should be given to

> Him who made His servant travel by night from the sacred place of worship to the farthest place of worship.

(surah 17:1)

The 'farthest place of worship' may mean either the holy city of Jerusalem or the presence of God in heaven.

The place from where Muslims believe the Prophet ascended to heaven

It is not clear whether this journey actually happened or was a vision. One tradition says that the Prophet, who had remarried, never left his sleeping wife's side. His body remained in Makkah while his spirit went to heaven. The Night Journey had a profound influence on the rest of his life.

THE JOURNEY

The angel Jibril shook the Prophet from sleep and took him to Jerusalem on a horse-like animal with wings, named *al-Buraq*, 'the Lightning'.

From Jerusalem he was taken through the seven heavens and shown paradise and hell. He met and spoke with earlier prophets, including Aaron, Musa, Ibrahim and Isa. He was surprised when he met Ibrahim, 'I never saw a man who looked so much like myself!'

THE PRAYERS

The Prophet was told how many times a Muslim should pray. The Prophet thought 50 times a day would be right. Musa said this would be too great a burden for ordinary humans. They settled on five, and that has remained Muslim practice ever since.

THE LIGHT

As the Prophet and the angel approached the highest heaven and the throne of God, Muhammad was aware of great peace and a brilliant, pure light. They could go no closer. Time, thought and feelings were stilled. The Prophet felt overwhelmed by the presence of God. He found it difficult to put such feelings into words.

> No vision can grasp Him, but His grasp is over all vision; He is above all comprehension, yet Himself knows all things.
>
> (surah 6:103)

> Those round the throne of God sing glory and praise to the Lord and believe in Him, and implore forgiveness for those who believe. Our Lord, Thy reach is over all things in mercy and knowledge.
>
> (surah 40:7)

All too soon it was ended, and the Prophet came back to earth. He was amazed to find the place where he had been sleeping was still warm, and a cup he tipped over was still emptying. It had all happened in a flash.

THE MEANING

For Muslims, the real meaning of this night was the inward and spiritual experience of the Prophet's ascent from earth to heaven.

Sufi mystics (see pages 148 and 152) insist that all believers *can* share this experience. This is the soul's journey when it leaves the human body behind and rises towards God, to the height of religious awareness.

After this experience, the Prophet felt great comfort and strength. He became convinced that God was always with him.

THINGS TO DO

1 One of the names of God is al-Latif – the One who cannot be imagined or understood. Why do you think this is?

2 Explain why Muslims think the Night Journey is the second most important time in the Prophet's life.

TALKING POINTS

- Many believers experience a time they describe as a 'dark night of the soul' before times of great spiritual awareness. Is it necessary to go through sorrow before you can fully know joy?

- Believers often speak of having seen the light. What is the 'darkness'? After such an experience, do you think the 'darkness' would:
  a seem darker
  b not matter at all or
  c be regretted, but no longer affect the believer?

FOR YOUR FOLDERS

1 What was the spiritual meaning of the Night Journey for Muslims?

2 Why would a Muslim be suspicious of anyone who claimed to 'know' God, or to be able to describe God?

THE CONVERTS OF YATHRIB

Yathrib was a town inhabited by three Arab tribes and two Jewish tribes. One day, pilgrims from Yathrib heard the Prophet preaching in Makkah and were very impressed. They invited him to go to their town with them.

They promised:

- to obey only Allah
- never to steal
- never to commit adultery
- never to do evil
- to protect the Prophet against all odds.

The Prophet warned them of dangers for those who responded to his call. They said they would accept all dangers but asked what reward they might expect for keeping their promises. He replied, 'Paradise!' The Prophet agreed to go with them to Yathrib.

THE HIJRAH

The **Hijrah** or Hegira is the name for the journey to Yathrib. The Prophet's followers went ahead but he stayed behind, waiting for God's final word to leave Makkah. He would be travelling alone. Tradition tells of a plot by his enemies who wanted to kill him. One member from each tribe would stab him, so that no individual could be blamed.

Ali stayed behind to act as decoy when the Prophet set out. The Prophet hid in a cave on **Mount Thawr** for four days. Abu Bakr's daughter, Asma, brought him food. A spider spun a web over the mouth of the cave, and a bird built a nest there. So even when his enemies were standing right outside the cave, they didn't suspect he was there.

THE ARRIVAL

When the Prophet arrived at Yathrib he had a wonderful welcome. Everyone wanted him to stay in their homes. He didn't want to give offence so said he would let his camel decide. The animal knelt at a place where dates were drying out. The Prophet bought the land and built a house there. This is preserved today as the first **mosque** or **masjid** (see page 110).

THE CALENDAR

Yathrib was re-named **Madinat-an-Nabi** (city of the Prophet, **nabi** means prophet) or **Madinah**. The Hijrah took place in 622 CE and this became the first year in the Muslim calendar. The Muslim calendar therefore numbers its years AH – after Hijrah.

ANSARS AND MUHAJIRUN

The Muslims who went with the Prophet had left everything behind and had no homes, little money and no employment. They were called **muhajirun**, or emigrants. The Prophet asked the people of Madinah for their help and support. They gave this without hesitation. Many took in individuals or even a whole family. These kind people became known as **ansars**, or helpers.

ORGANIZATION

For the next ten years the Prophet worked to unite the tribes under the rule of God. He was their political and religious leader.

- He drew up a constitution setting out the rights and duties of all the people in Madinah.
- He built the first mosque on his own land.
- He taught the people about regular prayer times.
- He organized collections of money for the poor, and taught his followers about regular fasting.

CONFLICTS

The Prophet still had enemies. The Makkans (people of Makkah) wanted him handed over, and some Jews were angry because they felt his message disagreed with their holy books.

The Prophet agreed that the Jewish prophets had received revelations from God. But he expected the Jews to become Muslims. However, the Treaty of Madinah protected the rights of Jews to practise their religion with total freedom as followers of the Prophet Musa (Moses). Muslims prayed facing Jerusalem and many fasted on the Jewish Day of Atonement.

> Say – 'We believe in the revelation which has come down to us and also in that which came down to you; Our God and your God is one and it is to Him that we bow.'
>
> (surah 29:46)

The Prophet soon received the revelation that Muslims should face Makkah when praying (surah 2:142–50), and that the fast on the Day of Atonement was voluntary. Muslims were to fast for the whole of the month of Ramadan.

Many Jews would not accept this new revelation so there was conflict between them and the Muslims. They sided with the traders in Makkah and tried to sabotage the Muslim way of life in Madinah.

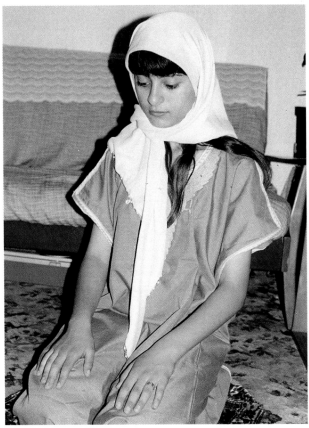

'O believer! Bow down and worship your Lord, and do good, that you may prosper.' (surah 22:77)

Brechin High School

FOR DISCUSSION

Muslims believe that loyalty to God comes before loyalty to their families. How might this:
a split families up
b bind them closer together?

THINKING POINTS

- Why do you think the Prophet expected the Jews of Madinah to become Muslim?

- Why do you think many were against him?

FOR YOUR FOLDERS

1 Write out the promises the converts of Madinah made.

2 How did the Prophet begin to organize the Muslims of Madinah?

MUHAMMAD THE RULER

The Prophet's family lived in simple houses

RULER OF MADINAH

Even after the Prophet became ruler of Madinah and had thousands of loyal followers, he still lived like a poor man. He used to work like his friends. He mended his own clothes, repaired his shoes, did the shopping and milked the goats.

He could have lived in luxury like a king. But he believed there was no king but God. He believed that it was wrong to be greedy and keep more than he needed. This would show lack of faith in God the Provider.

He believed that everything belongs to God. Therefore, if the Prophet received money or goods, he gave them away again, to be shared among the poor and needy people.

God must come first. A Muslim must give up all he had for God. To do less meant that love of things came before the love of God. A person could only show true submission by giving up everything.

The Prophet taught that it wasn't hard to give up or go without things for God, because it was done out of great love for God.

The Prophet's 'kingdom' was ruled by God. All the subjects agreed to accept God's laws and not the wishes of human rulers.

LAWS FOR MUSLIMS

Here are some of the laws.

- Control your anger, then forgive your brother.
- Do not hate each other, envy each other or provoke each other.
- Do not spy on each other or betray each other's trust.
- Do not speak ill of your friend behind his back.
- Give the labourer his wages before his sweat dries.
- Do not drink alcohol, and do not gamble. It opens the door to the devil.
- Do not steal the property of another.
- Do not cheat each other.
- Do not defile (spoil) the honour of a woman.
- Do not charge interest on money loaned to those who need it.
- Do not reveal your friend's weaknesses.
- Do not pay bribes to get what is not lawfully yours.
- Do not commit adultery or practise homosexuality.
- Do not be cruel to slaves, or forbid them to marry or to buy their freedom.
- Do not force slaves into sexual relationships they do not desire.
- Do not kill unwanted babies, either before or after birth, because of poverty.
- Do not be cruel to animals.

SLAVERY

At that time, slavery was lawful. However, the Prophet hoped that the time would come when slavery would no longer exist, and the whole community would look after poor people.

THE PROPHET'S SIMPLE LIFE

Muhammad lived a very simple life. He ate very little and sometimes had no hot food at all. Some days he took nothing but water. He thought it was weakness to give in to the desire to comfort the body.

He owned only one change of clothes, which he carefully mended and patched. He used his cloak as a blanket at night. One story tells of a cat that brought her kittens and settled on a corner of the cloak. In the morning, he cut off the piece of fabric and made sure they stayed warm and cosy.

RULES ABOUT WIVES

It was the custom at that time for men to have many wives. The prophet **Dawud** (King David) had ten, his son **Suleimen** (King Solomon) kept 1000 women. Men could have as many women as they could afford. If they got tired of one, they could just throw her out. Under the Qur'an, the marriage laws were changed to give some protection to women.

After the death of Khadijah, the Prophet took in twelve other women. These were daughters of friends, widows of soldiers and daughters of defeated enemies. Other Muslim men were allowed to support up to four women, but only if all were willing. They had to be treated equally (see units 50–51).

THE PROPHET'S HOME LIFE

The Prophet's house was made up of a row of small rooms for himself and his wives. His only furniture was a leather sack filled with branches and leaves to lean against, and a rush mat to sleep on. He never slept in a soft bed. He often stood in prayer the whole night, sometimes with his youngest wife **Aishah**. His wives accepted the simple life and were devoted to God. They were known to be kind and generous, and Muslims called them 'mothers of the faithful'. The Prophet was also very fond of children, especially his grandchildren. He would even interrupt his prayers to play with them.

The Prophet's way of life, or example, is known as the **Sunnah**. Muslims who follow Sunnah are known as **Sunni** Muslims (see unit 72).

FOR YOUR FOLDERS

Read the list of laws the Prophet expected Muslims to obey.

1 Write down the *ten* laws that you think are most important.

2 Explain why you chose those laws.

THINGS TO DO

Which of the laws for Muslims would be most difficult to keep:

a for a nosy, bad-tempered person

b for an employer

c for a wealthy business person

d for you?

FOR DISCUSSION

Why do you think the Prophet chose a simple life when he could have had all the riches and luxuries he wanted?

In the new Islamic state of Madinah, all the citizens had equal rights. The Prophet taught that God judged a person's worth according to their heart.

> The most noble among you in the sight of God is the one who is most virtuous.
>
> (surah 49:13)

Few of the Muslims were wealthy because they arrived from Makkah with nothing. The people of Madinah (Madinans) took them in and looked after them. The Prophet told them that what mattered was the strength of their faith, not their wealth.

THE BATTLE OF BADR

The Makkans still wanted to harm the Prophet. They tried to bribe the Madinans to hand him over. They persecuted the families of Muslims who remained in Makkah and took their property. In 623 CE a small group of Muslims raided a Makkan camel train. The Prophet did not order the attack, though he understood why it took place. Sadly it gave the Makkans reason to attack Madinah with their army.

Abu Sufyan, a relative of the Prophet who opposed him, set out with 1000 men. The Prophet only had 313 warriors, including young boys. They marched out of the city and camped at **al-Badr**. They were willing to die for God if they had to.

To everyone's amazement, the Prophet's men won. The Makkan army fled, leaving 70 of their men killed and 70 as prisoners. The Muslims became known as a victorious military power whom Allah protected.

THE BATTLE OF UHUD

The Makkans attacked the Muslims at **Mount Uhud** the next year. The Muslims lost the battle this time. They had lacked discipline. The Prophet was injured – he lost two teeth.

The Muslims were depressed. They thought God had deserted them. Later, it was seen as a test.

> Your courage failed, there was chaos, and they disobeyed the Prophet. God allowed you to be defeated in order to test you.
>
> (surah 3:152)

When Muslims acted according to revelation (see unit 4) they succeeded, but when they acted on a human level, they made mistakes.

It was revealed to the Prophet that:

- it was acceptable to defend the faith in battle
- Muslims who died fighting for God would go straight to paradise
- the wars were God's will and the Muslim soldiers were God's army.

> Fight in the cause of God those who fight you, but do not go beyond the limits. Slay them whenever you find them, and remove them from the places they forced you to leave; for tyranny and oppression are worse than murder. Don't fight at the sacred mosque unless they fight you there [first] – but if they do, then slay them. Such is the reward of those who suppress faith. But if they stop, remember God is the Forgiving, the Merciful.
>
> (surah 2:190–2)

After more battles, in 629 CE the Prophet had a dream telling him to go unarmed on a pilgrimage to Makkah. He went with 1400 men. The Makkans came out to fight, but when they saw he came in peace, they agreed to a ten-year truce. The Makkans broke this truce the next year, but by then 2000 Muslims had made their pilgrimage to Makkah.

MUHAMMAD TAKES MAKKAH

In 630 CE the Prophet took an army of 10 000 men to Makkah. He met only slight resistance. He circled round the Ka'bah seven times and touched the Black Stone set in a corner of the Ka'bah (see unit 35). Then he called everyone to midday prayer. Makkah had been conquered in the name of Allah, and only eleven people had been killed.

As a conqueror he was kind and forgiving. He gave a free pardon to all his enemies. Soon everyone in Makkah became Muslim. After this Makkah became the Muslim holy city and nobody who was not a Muslim was allowed to enter it. This ban still holds today.

From the disorder and evil that he knew when he began his work, the Prophet had established a well-disciplined state in the name of Allah. There was justice and compassion instead of oppression and unkindness. Muslims now longed for the submission of the whole world to Allah.

Muslims fight to bring justice

TALKING POINTS

- Belief in peace at all costs might be a temptation to cowardice.

- Defence is not the same as attack.

- Being prepared to sacrifice yourself because of your belief in non-violence may not bring about a just peace.

FOR YOUR FOLDERS

1 Read surah 2:190–2 then answer these questions.

   a When should Muslims fight?

   b What is 'worse than murder'?

2 'The battles of holy war are not against people, but against evil.' Do you think this is true? Explain your answer.

3 How did the Prophet show that he was a forgiving conqueror?

THINKING POINTS

Muslims do not believe in peace at all costs. They think it is sometimes wrong *not* to fight. Here are some examples where they would think it would be right to take action:

- someone is beating up an old person or a child

- someone is attacking your mother, brother or sister

- a teacher sees a bully torment a child.

The Mount of Mercy, where the Prophet gave his final sermon

Today I have perfected your religion for you, completed My favour upon you, and have chosen for you Islam as the way of your life.

(surah 5:4 – the last revelation given to the Prophet)

In 632 CE the Prophet went back to Makkah on a pilgrimage, with a crowd of about 140 000 people. He went up the Mount of Mercy and preached a great sermon.

THE SERMON

O people, listen to my words carefully… You must live at peace with one another. Everyone must respect the rights and property of their neighbours. There must be no rivalry or enmity among you. Just as you regard this month as sacred, so regard the life and property of every Muslim in the same way. Remember, you will surely appear before God and answer for your actions.

All believers are brothers…you are not allowed to take things from another Muslim unless he gives it to you willingly. You are to look after your families with all your heart and be kind to the women God has entrusted to you.

You have been left God's Book, the Qur'an. If you hold fast to it and do not let it go you will not stray from the right path…I leave behind me two things, the Qur'an and the example of my life. If you follow these you will not fail.

Listen to me very carefully. Worship God, be steadfast in prayer, fast during Ramadan, pay alms to the less fortunate.

People, no prophet or messenger will come after me, and no new faith will emerge. All those who listen to me will pass on my words to others, and those to others again.

(Hadith)

At the end of the speech he looked round at the crowd. 'Have I fulfilled my mission?' he cried. The crowd roared back, 'You have fulfilled it, O messenger of God.'

Muhammad called out three times, 'O God, You are Witness.' The crowd was silent. Then Bilal's powerful voice called the faithful to prayer, and they all joined in worshipping God.

DEATH OF MUHAMMAD

When Muhammad returned to Madinah he became ill with a fever and violent headaches. He moved into Aishah's room to be nursed until he died.

He was too ill to reach the praying place outside, so he asked Abu Bakr to lead prayers in his place.

On his last day, after the dawn prayer, he lay back, exhausted, in Aishah's arms. His head grew heavy and she heard him say, 'Lord, grant me pardon.' His last words were, 'I have chosen the most exalted company, in paradise.' With that, the Prophet died.

Umar, the close friend of Muhammad, refused to believe that the Prophet could die. He thought he would live for ever. Abu Bakr reminded the people that they must not worship the Prophet.

Muhammad is but a messenger; there have been many prophets before him, and they all died. If he dies or is killed, will you now turn back?

(surah 3:144)

Tradition suggests that Muhammad died on 8 June 632 CE at the age of 63. He was buried where he died in Aishah's room. His grave is still a place of pilgrimage today. Muslims regard him as the greatest of all men, 'the seal of the prophets', the servant and messenger of God.

THINKING POINT

If all [the waters of] the sea were ink [with which to write] the words of my Lord, the sea would surely be drained before his words are finished, even if we were to add to it sea upon sea.

(surah 18:109)

FOR YOUR FOLDERS

1 A seal is the 'stamp of approval' or guarantee on a document. Why do you think Muhammad was called the 'seal of the prophets'?

2 Write a list of the personal qualities that a great leader must have. To what extent do you think the Prophet possessed these?

TALKING POINT

'The Prophet Muhammad could not have been successful if he lived in our time.' Do you agree? Give reasons for your answer.

WHAT MUSLIMS BELIEVE ABOUT GOD

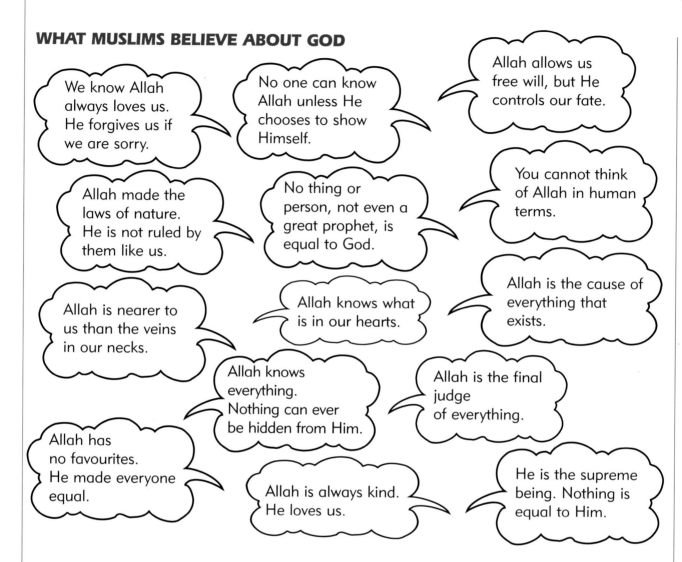

We know Allah always loves us. He forgives us if we are sorry.

No one can know Allah unless He chooses to show Himself.

Allah allows us free will, but He controls our fate.

Allah made the laws of nature. He is not ruled by them like us.

No thing or person, not even a great prophet, is equal to God.

You cannot think of Allah in human terms.

Allah is nearer to us than the veins in our necks.

Allah knows what is in our hearts.

Allah is the cause of everything that exists.

Allah knows everything. Nothing can ever be hidden from Him.

Allah is the final judge of everything.

Allah has no favourites. He made everyone equal.

Allah is always kind. He loves us.

He is the supreme being. Nothing is equal to Him.

Many people live their entire lives without ever thinking about the reason for their existence. They think the world they live in is all there is. Their lives are just something to pass through until everything stops at death.

Muslims think that it is impossible for anything just to come into existence from nothing. They believe that God has given some people (the prophets) special understanding.

Muslims also believe that our conscience is there to encourage us to improve ourselves and to stop us from doing wrong. These things help them to conclude that *there is a god*.

Muslims believe that a person will reach paradise if they recognize that God exists, and that He is above and beyond all the things that He has created. Without this understanding, a person cannot enter paradise. It is not that God is unkind in refusing to allow a person into paradise. Rather, if a person refuses to accept God's loving presence, then a wall is built separating the person from God. Nothing can be done until the 'wall' is taken away.

THE LIGHT

God is the light of the heavens and the earth; His light may be compared to a niche in which there is a lamp; the lamp is in a crystal; the crystal is…a glittering star kindled from a blessed olive tree neither of the East nor of the West. Its oil would burst into flames even though fire had hardly touched it; Light upon Light!

(surah 24:35)

Those who believe in the Qur'an and those who follow the Jewish scriptures and the Christians and the Sabians…who believe in God and the Last Day and do good works shall have their reward with their Lord; on them shall be no fear, nor shall they grieve.

(surah 2:62)

It is He who sends down blessings upon you as do His angels, that He may bring you out of the darkness into the light. He is full of mercy to those who believe; on the day they meet Him the cry will be of 'Peace', and He has prepared for them a generous reward.

(surah 33:43–4)

He will provide for you a Light by which you will walk [straight on your path]; He will forgive [your past], for God always forgives and is most merciful.

(surah 57:28)

O God, who knows the innermost secrets of our hearts – lead us out of the darkness into the light.

(Prayer of the Prophet)

Allah, the name of God, in Arabic script

FOR YOUR FOLDERS

1 What reasons help Muslims to decide that God exists?

2 Why do you think some people do not believe that God exists?

3 Are some people more 'religious' than others? Give reasons for your answer.

THINGS TO DO

1 Read the words about light. Why do you think God is compared with light.

2 Make two lists headed 'Light' and 'Darkness'. Put experiences or emotions that you think should go in each list.

3 Choose five of the statements about God and write them out on a decorated scroll or poster.

God's guidance is often compared to light

TAWHID

Muslims use the word **Tawhid** to express the 'oneness' or unity of God. It means that there is one God, alone and without equal. Muslims believe that there is nothing to which you can compare God.

> He is Allah, the One, Allah is Eternal and Absolute. None is born of Him, He is unborn. There is none like unto Him.
>
> (surah 112)

TRANSCENDENCE

Tawhid is the belief that God alone is the power that created the universe and guides it in its path. God knows everything, sees everything and can do anything.

God is transcendent. This means that He is outside and beyond the created world and time. He is not bound by the same limits as humans. God is infinite and eternal – He does not have a beginning or an end. When Muslims think of God in this way, they feel He is beyond human knowledge and reasoning.

> No vision can grasp Him, but His grasp is over all vision; He is above all comprehension, yet [knows] all things.
>
> (surah 6:103)

IMMANENCE

Muslims also believe that God is **immanent**. This means that He is present everywhere within the universe. He is closer to each human than their heartbeat and knows their secret thoughts.

> When my servants ask you about Me I am close [to them]; I listen to the prayer of every one who calls to Me. Let them listen to Me and believe in Me, that they may walk in the right way.
>
> (surah 2:186)

Muslims believe God listens to every prayer

BREAKING TAWHID

Tawhid sums up the Muslim outlook on life. The following sins break Tawhid.

- To think that you 'own' anything: everything in the universe belongs to God: humans only 'borrow' possessions, or even their own bodies, for as long as God allows it.

- Pride or arrogance: God gave you your talents or brain capacity before you were born – you did not choose them.

- Ignorance of God's supremacy: there is no other power like God's. Superstition breaks Tawhid.

- Complaining to God or asking Him to change His will to suit you better: God is just and compassionate (kind). If we suffer, it is for a reason – even if we do not understand it.

- Thinking you can fool God: He knows even your subconscious thoughts!

- False pride or sense of holiness (hypocrisy): God is not fooled by this.

SHIRK

The sin of **shirk** is comparing God to any created thing, or to say that other things or people somehow share in His creative power, or have His knowledge or ability to guide or forgive.

For Muslims, the Holy Spirit is God in action, not a separate being.

The idea that God could join with a human to produce a being that was half-human and half-divine, is blasphemy (an insult to God) for Muslims.

A prophet cannot be God. Muslims believe that Isa was the greatest and most humble of prophets before Muhammad. 'The miracle worker' – who even raised the dead – was a supreme Muslim and not a divine being. They believe that Isa never claimed to be God and that these claims were made by Christians after his death.

Muslims accept that Isa was born of a virgin mother and worked miracles. This was revealed to the Prophet in the Qur'an. But they do not believe God and Isa were equal (see unit 17).

RESULTS

Belief in Tawhid results in:

- *faith* and surrender to the will of Allah
- *self-respect* and *confidence:* Muslims depend on and fear no one but God
- *humility* and *modesty:* whatever Muslims are or own comes from God, so they cannot be proud or boastful
- *responsibility*, because Muslims know they must answer to God for their actions
- *trust*, because they believe that everything is God's will and therefore was planned
- *courage*, because they know they will not die before the appointed time for them to do so
- *unity with the universe*, because they act for God in taking care of the planet
- *determination* and *patience*, because Muslims have the difficult task of pleasing God.

O people of the Book!…The Messiah, Isa, son of Maryam, was [only] an apostle of God, and His word which He conveyed to Maryam, and a spirit proceeding from Himself. Say not 'Three' …God is only one God. Far be it from His glory that He should have a son.

(surah 4:171)

FOR DISCUSSION

Why do Muslims believe it is impossible to describe God in human terms?

FOR YOUR FOLDERS

1 Explain the meaning of transcendent, immanent and hypocrisy.
2 Write a list of what Muslims believe are the most important results of Tawhid in their lives. You could do this as a diagram or pattern, just using the key words.
3 How do you think pride, envy, hatred or selfishness would break Tawhid?
4 Explain what is meant by the sin of shirk.

THINGS TO DO

Copy out one of the surah quotations given in this unit and explain what you think it means.

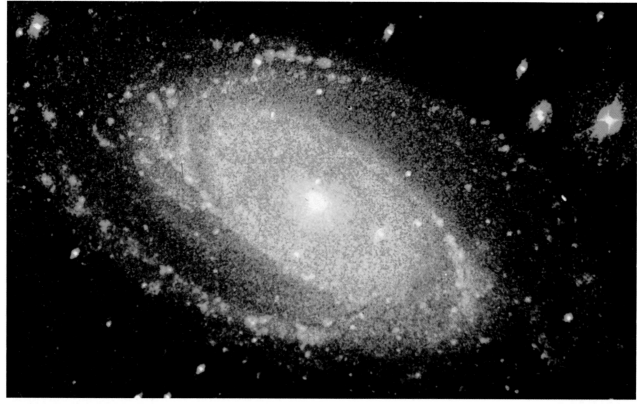

'Allah is Lord of all the worlds' (surah 1:2)

THINKING ABOUT CREATION

Interviewer: Ali, why do you think Allah created all this? How can you prove it?

Ali: The universe didn't just spring into being by accident. Some scientists say that sort of thing because they don't want to believe in God. But they can't give the answer. They're only guessing.

Interviewer: But they know what they're talking about.

Ali: Look, isn't it possible that this whole universe might never have existed at all?

Interviewer: I suppose so.

Ali: Well, *you* might never have existed. That table might never have existed. Nothing exists without a cause. Therefore, if the universe *does* exist, it must be because of a reason. If you take away the cause, how can anything happen?

Interviewer: Can we prove God exists, then, from the laws of nature? Maybe God just evolved?

Ali: How can God be under the same rules as that which He created? He is above and beyond them.

Interviewer: Don't you think scientists will ever prove the existence of God then?

Ali: How can a creature who only sees black and white understand what is meant by 'blue'? You can show a monkey all the rules of science but it won't understand them. A human being will never fully understand the universe – let alone Allah who made it.

Interviewer: Are scientists just wasting their time then?

Ali: No, no. They make discoveries all the time. Allah wants us to be intelligent and to love Him. But look at all these rules the scientists discover – they're nothing *new*, are they? Science just suddenly sees what has always been there. A true scientist realizes they don't know very much.

Interviewer: That's true! Our great scientist Sir Isaac Newton once said that after his whole lifetime's study, he had been just like a boy playing with pebbles on the beach.

Ali: In any case, the universe contains far more than our own solar system. There's the whole of space out there, whole regions of existence, whole heavens waiting to be explored.

Interviewer: Will we ever know the truth, Ali?

Ali: One day, maybe. Insha Allah [if God wills].

> There is no God but He, the Living, the Self-Subsisting, the Eternal. He neither slumbers nor sleeps…No person can grasp anything of His knowledge, except as God wills it.
>
> (surah 2:255)

> God has the key of the unseen, the treasures none know but He. He knows whatever is on land and in the sea; no leaf falls without His knowing it; there is not a grain in the darkness of earth, or a green or dry thing, but it is carefully noted.
>
> (surah 6:59)

> To God belong the East and the West; wherever you turn, there is the Presence of God; for God is All-Pervading, All-Knowing.
>
> (surah 2:115)

> False Gods cannot create a fly – nor could they ever get back what a fly could take from them.
>
> (surah 22:73)

THE SEVEN HEAVENS

Muslims believe there are seven heavens beyond our universe. These are the seven heavens the Prophet saw on his Night Journey (see unit 6). In the heavens he met Adam, Ibrahim, Musa and Isa.

As he drew nearer to God, he found himself surrounded by 'Oceans' of light and felt a sense of perfect peace.

FOR YOUR FOLDERS

1 Explain why Muslims believe that:

a the universe did not happen by accident

b there is evidence for the existence of God.

2 Read the surahs on this page. Explain what you think each one teaches about God.

THINGS TO DO

1 Look up and write out the meanings of these names of Allah:

Compassionate; Supreme; Omnipotent; Omnipresent; Omniscient; Beneficent.

2 Work out what 'causes' a table to exist. (The table exists because, first of all…)

3 Love is known by its effects. Write down some of the effects of love that prove it actually exists.

TALKING POINTS

1 Does a living cell in your body know that you exist?

2 Do the mind or conscience actually exist? Or are these simply the workings of the brain?

3 Why do Muslims believe human beings can never really understand their Creator?

He sends forth guardians [to watch] over you, and when death overtakes you, the messengers will carry away your soul.

(surah 6:61)

Behold two guardians appointed to learn his doings, one sitting on his right hand and one on the left.

(surah 50:17)

BEINGS IN THE UNIVERSE

Muslims believe that beings other than humans and animals exist in the universe. They believe in non-human beings called **jinn** and angels. Because they are not human, they are beyond human understanding. Muslims object strongly to any attempt to draw pictures of these.

Jinn are thought of as spirits, neither good nor evil. The Qur'an describes them as being made from fire. They can upset or disturb humans, but can also be friendly and kind. Surah 72 mentions some who were converted to Islam.

Angels are the messengers of God. They help people to become aware of God.

Neither angels nor jinn have physical bodies, but they can have an effect on material things and on the people with whom they come into contact. Humans and jinn have free-will (they can choose their actions), but angels *always* follow the will of God.

ANGELS

'Angel' means 'messenger'. This is their main task. Muslims believe that angels are creatures of light who occupy the whole universe. They are specially close when a person prays or thinks about God. Then their loving presence brings a feeling of peace and helps to make worship more meaningful.

PROTECTING FRIENDS

Surely those who say: 'Our Lord is Allah' and then go straight, the angels descend upon them saying: 'Fear not and do not be sad, and hear the good news about the Garden which you have been promised. We are your protecting friends in the life of this world, and in the next world.'

(surah 41:30–1)

Muslims believe that humans occasionally see angels at times of great crisis. Sometimes very sensitive people become aware of a loving presence guiding them and watching over their lives.

An angel may take human shape, as Jibril did to the prophet Ibrahim and to Maryam, the mother of Isa. But it can take any shape it pleases. According to Hadith, Muhammad first saw Jibril as a huge creature with thousands of wings covering the horizon between heaven and earth.

NAMED ANGELS

Jibril – the messenger of God who gives revelations to chosen ones
Azra'il – the angel of death who receives the souls of the dying
Israfil – calls all souls on the Day of Judgement
Mika'il – protector of the faithful and guardian of the places of worship
Munker and Nadir – will question souls
Iblis – the devil or **Shaytan** – chief of the jinn

THE DEVIL

Muslims believe that angels and jinn existed before evil did, when the universe was perfect. The urge to do evil began when humans were created. God intended the first man, Adam, to rule the earth and look after it.

He ordered all the angels to respect this – and almost all of them did. But Iblis (also called Satan or Shaytan) refused to obey because he thought he was a superior creature.

God punished him for this, so he became the enemy of all humans. Since that time he has tried to lead people away from God. 'Iblis' means 'desperate' and 'Satan' means someone who plots against another.

> The Lord said to the angels…'When I have created Man and breathed My spirit into him, then fall ye down and worship him.' So all the angels bowed down in worship…But not so Iblis (the chief jinn): he refused to be among those who bowed down.
>
> (surah 15:28–31)

THE RECORD

Muslims believe that every person has two special angels, or guardians, who keep a record of their good and bad deeds. Nothing a person does or thinks is ever unknown, unseen, forgotten or left out.

At the end of formal prayers Muslims turn to the right and the left, and bless their two angels (see unit 27).

Muslims bless their two angels after formal prayers

THINKING POINTS

- Think over your last *two* days. Make a list of some of your good and bad thoughts and actions that might have gone into your angels' record books.
- Do you think a Muslim can be helped by a belief in guardians? Give reasons for your answer.

TALKING POINTS

- Do we need to have 'evil' for us to know what 'good' is?
- 'The universe only contains creatures proved to exist by science. Belief in angels is just imagination.' Do you agree?

FOR YOUR FOLDERS

1 Why do Muslims believe that evil is possible in a universe created by God, who is good?

2 'Pride and disobedience are real causes of evil.' Do you think this is true? Give reasons for your answer.

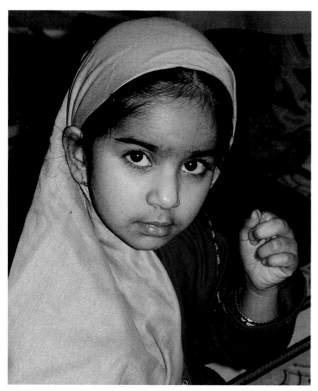

It is the soul that is the real person

SOIL

Muslims believe that all human beings are descendants of Adam and **Eve**. God created this original couple. 'Adam' means 'soil' or 'dust' and 'Eve' comes from a word meaning 'living'.

Our physical bodies are made of 'clay'. Our human nature depends on humus, the living part of soil. Bodies are what they eat, that is they need to take in the fruits of the earth. If they stop – they die.

GOD'S IMAGE

Muslims do not believe that God made humans to look like him. He may not 'look like' *any* of the things He has created.

Muslims do not believe that humans evolved or descended from apes. Apes were created as apes: humans as humans. They believe that the theory of evolution is only a theory and not a proven fact.

We created Man from the essence [of clay]; We made out of that lump bones and clothed the bones with flesh; then We developed out of it another creature.

(surah 23:12–15)

O Humanity, be mindful of your duty to God, who created you from a single soul, and from it created its mate, and from the two spread widely many men and women.

(surah 4:1)

THE SOUL

Human beings are the highest of God's creations. They have freedom of will and action. They can decide their own future. They can reproduce themselves, just as other animals do. However, Muslims believe that God gave to each human being a separate, individual soul, called the **ruh**. It is the soul that is the real person, not the body that the soul lives in.

THE TIME SPAN

Muslims believe that God allows each soul to live in a body for a certain time, until it is taken away. Muslims believe that each soul belongs to an individual person. It does not travel into another person's body, or an animal's. It is not reincarnated to live again on earth. Although the body breaks down after death, a person's soul and body will be reunited when the Hour of Judgement comes.

Some say, 'What is there but our life in this world? We live and we die, and only Time destroys us.' In this they have no knowledge, it is merely their own guesswork. God gives you life, then causes you to die; then He will assemble you again on the Day of Judgement.

(surah 45:24)

ALL EQUAL

Because human beings have conscious souls they can be loving and kind – or hateful and destructive. Therefore humans do not remain equal. The spiritual nature of human beings raises them above the animal kingdom, and makes them responsible for it. But some humans behave so badly, they sink below the level of animals.

> We have honoured the sons of Adam, provided them with transport on land and sea, given them for food things good and pure, and conferred on them special favours above a great part of Our creation.
>
> (surah 17:70)

KHILAFAH – STEWARDSHIP

Muslims believe that Allah gave human beings the ability to think rationally, and a sense of responsibility. He also required them to be guardians of the planet on His behalf – His deputies or **khalifahs**.

Muslims make a great effort to look after the world (see unit 45). They accept the duty to look after other people, especially those who are less fortunate than themselves. They work to preserve the earth's species and to ensure the proper use of the earth's resources.

> Be steadfast in prayer and regular in charity;…for God sees all that you do.
>
> (surah 2:110)

THINGS TO DO

1 Read the surahs in this unit. What do they say about the beginning, lifetime and end of humans?

2 What is a khalifah? How could you be a khalifah in your own lifetime?

THINKING POINTS

- How dependent on the earth (and its produce) is a physical body? What happens to the body after death?

- What is it that makes a 'person'? Think about the changes in physical appearance due to age (baby to adult; adult to old age), or accidents or operations – yet the 'person' remains the same.

FOR YOUR FOLDERS

1 Explain what Muslims believe about the creation of humans and other species.

2 Why do Muslims believe the physical body is not the real person?

3 What do Muslims believe happens to a person after death?

QUICK QUIZ

1 Who was the first man?

2 What do the names Adam and Eve mean?

3 What was Adam made out of?

4 What is the ruh?

5 What is the soul's time-span?

6 When are soul and body reunited?

Some people are chosen as prophets

GOD'S DUTY

Muslims believe that it is a person's duty to love and serve God and submit to His will. But how can a person decide whether an action is right or wrong?

Since God is just, clearly it is His duty to reveal His will to us and give us a code of conduct by which to live.

Risalah is the means by which God communicates with human beings. A **rasul** is a prophet. When God communicates directly to a prophet's mind, this is called revelation.

THE MESSENGERS

Long before Muhammad became the Prophet, God communicated with many other people. Muslims believe the first prophet was Adam, and that between Adam and Muhammad there were thousands of other messengers. The Qur'an mentions at least 24 of them. God has always revealed Himself to those who were spiritual enough to understand His messages.

Messengers did not choose this work. God chose them, sometimes to their surprise and reluctance. God didn't choose people who were rich and famous. He chose those who lived good and honourable lives.

The five great prophets before Muhammad were: Adam, **Nuh** (Noah), Ibrahim (Abraham), Musa (Moses) and Isa (Jesus).

> God chooses for Himself whoever He pleases, and guides to Himself those who turn [to him].
>
> (surah 42:13)

THE SEAL

The Prophet Muhammad is special for Muslims because he was the last of the prophets. He was the final seal of all those who had gone before.

THE BOOKS

The holy books include the:

- **Sahifa** – the scrolls given to Ibrahim
- **Tawrah** – the revelation to Musa (the Torah)
- **Zabur** – the psalms given to Dawud (David)
- **Injil** – the teachings given to Isa (the Gospels).

However, Muslims believe the books and teachings were not preserved in their original form. Sahifa was lost completely, and Zabur, Tawrah and Injil were changed in various ways.

Muslims believe the Injil is not the same as the Gospels that Christians use in Church.

The Tawrah is not the same as the present Torah of the Jews. They believe that many comments, opinions, legends and other things were added later by editors. It is very difficult to get at the truth.

Muslims therefore accept Jewish and Christian scriptures only as edited versions of the revelation. They believe the guidance they contain cannot always be trusted.

THE QUR'AN

What the Prophet saw and heard was different. It was the *complete guidance*, the last 'revealed book'. Muslims call it **Umm-ul-Kitab** or 'Mother of Books' – meaning the greatest of all books.

Muslims believe the revelations given to the Prophet were intended to be preserved exactly. They were given to put right any errors in previous holy books. They were a message not just for Arabs but for the whole of humanity.

All the parts of the Qur'an were written down during the Prophet's lifetime. They were carefully checked several times. The Qur'an exists today in its original form, unaltered.

THE ORDER

The order of the surahs in the Qur'an is not the order in which the Prophet received them. Muslims believe that God told the Prophet the order towards the end of his life. Tradition says that the angel Jibril made the Prophet repeat all the surahs in the order God wanted, once every year, and twice in the year he died.

For Muslims, the Qur'an is the greatest of miracles. It is the exact message of God and its words must never be altered. They try to encourage all believers to study it in Arabic, the original language. This is because all translations differ and none can give the exact meaning of the original.

17 ISA (JESUS)

DISCUSSING ISA (PEACE BE UPON HIM)

Interviewer: Tell me, Hassan, is it true that Muslims believe in Jesus?

Hassan: Yes – but not in the same way that a Christian does. We show him more respect in many ways than Christians do!

Interviewer: What do you mean?

Hassan: Isa is revealed in the Qur'an so no one would mock him or doubt his miraculous birth. You won't hear Muslims using the name of Isa as bad language.

Interviewer: You believe in the virgin birth of Isa?

Hassan. Certainly! Maryam is mentioned more times in the Qur'an than in the New Testament. To say Maryam was not a virgin is blasphemy to a Muslim. It is an insult to God.

Interviewer: Why?

Hassan: Because there is no limit to the power of God.

Interviewer: But do you believe Isa was the son of God?

Hassan: Only in the way that we are all God's children. Isa is not God. He is our brother. Remember, Adam had no father *or* mother, so his birth was an even greater miracle. But no one claims he was equal with God or part of a Trinity.

Interviewer: Do you believe in the crucifixion?

Hassan: Yes – *a* crucifixion. But we don't think it was Isa who died. We think God took him up to heaven without letting him die at all – the Ascension. We don't believe God allowed the Jews or the Romans to kill him.

Interviewer: So you don't believe he died to save people from their sins?

Hassan: No. Christians seem to think the only reason they will be forgiven is because Isa 'paid the price' for them. We say that God is the Compassionate, the Merciful. If we turn to God for forgiveness, He will surely forgive us. We have free will – we can choose God or not. But we must pay the penalty ourselves. In any case, how can God send Himself to earth and kill Himself to save us? It doesn't make sense.

Interviewer: But don't you believe in the teachings of Isa then?

Hassan: Yes! But we think the Christian holy books were not written by Isa himself. His followers, who didn't really understand his relationship with God, wrote them, then they were edited. The revelation in the Qur'an is clear – it comes straight from God.

Interviewer: One of the sayings of Isa is 'No one goes to the Father except by me.' (John 14:6).

Hassan: It also says '…no one can come to me unless the Father makes it possible for him to do so.' (John 6:65).

Interviewer: I see what you mean… .

Hassan: I like the prayer of Isa best – 'Our Father, who art in Heaven' – that's pure Islam. We worship God *with* Isa. He is our brother.

ISA SUBMITS TO GOD

> She said, 'How, O Lord, shall I have a son, when no man has ever touched me?'
> He said, 'Thus: God creates what He wills. He says no more than "Be!" and it is so.'
>
> (surah 3:47)

> His name shall be Messiah Isa, the son of Maryam, held in honour in this world and the next; one of those nearest to God.
>
> (surah 3:45)

> And they crucified him not, but only one who was made to appear to them like Isa …They did not really kill Isa, but God took him up to Himself.
>
> (surah 4:157–8)

ISA THE HEALER

Isa, on whom be peace, saw a blind leper who was saying: 'Praise be to God, who has saved me from so many things.' 'From what are you free?' Isa asked him. 'Spirit of God,' said the wretched man, 'I am better off than those who do not know God.' 'You speak truly', said Isa. 'Stretch out your hand.' He was instantly restored to health, through the power of God. And he followed Isa and worshipped with him.

(story preserved by the Muslim teacher **al-Ghazzali**, from *Elephant in the Dark* by Idries Shah, Octagon Press, 1978)

THINKING POINT

Is it possible for one person to suffer or to pay the penalty for another person's sin?

FOR YOUR FOLDERS

Why don't Muslims believe that Isa's death was to 'pay the price' for the sins of humanity?

THINGS TO DO

Copy out these statements and tick the ones Muslims would agree with.

- Isa was miraculously born to the Virgin Maryam.
- Isa was God made man.
- Isa was the expected Messiah.
- Isa died on the cross.
- Isa died to save us from our sins.
- Everyone pays the penalty for their own sins.
- Isa ascended into heaven.
- Isa was 'of one substance with the Father, by whom all things were made' (from a Christian creed).
- Isa was a prophet, the miracle worker.
- Isa prayed to 'Our Father in Heaven'.
- Isa could have said, 'No one can come to the Father except through me.'

Isa, the miracle worker, heals a blind man

CAUSE AND EFFECT

Imagine you didn't know what an acorn was and you had never seen an oak tree. You would never guess what the acorn would become. If you saw the oak tree, you would never guess what it had come from.

What about yourself? It seems strange that the whole person that is you was once just a tiny 'seed' and 'seed receiver'. And who knows what you still may become?

The whole universe is like that. It is about cause and effect. We might know something about it, but we don't know much! Muslims believe the whole creation was *caused* by God.

AL-QADR

Muslims believe that Allah knows everything in the smallest detail. He knows how many leaves there are on a tree, or how many hairs there are on your head.

Everything that exists or happens has a purpose. Everything is part of His plan for His creation and is under His control.

Al-Qadr, which means 'destiny', is the Muslim belief that everything is planned by God. There cannot be such things as chance or random events.

> Whatever God grants to humanity out of His mercy, no one can withhold; and what He withholds no one can grant apart from Him.
>
> (surah 35:2)

> If God lay the touch of trouble on you, no one can deliver you from it save God alone; and if He wills good for you, no one can prevent His blessing. He confers them on His servants as He chooses.
>
> (surah 10:107)

We do not know our destiny but we have the free will to choose

INSTINCT AND MIND

All humans have instinct (called **nafs**). They are also free to choose good or evil. The part that makes the choice is the mind. Muslims believe God does not control anyone's mind, but allows them *free will*.

Allah already knows our mind before we do. Our destiny is already known. He knows if we are going to obey or disobey His will, but that doesn't take away our freedom. Humans do not know their destiny, and can still choose what they will do.

> On the Day of Judgement no step of a servant of God shall slip until he has answered concerning four things:
> – his body and how he used it
> – his life and how he spent it
> – his wealth and how he earned it
> – his knowledge and what he did with it.
>
> (Hadith)

FREE WILL

Freedom of choice places great responsibility on a person. God could have made us all into robots, but He did not do so. We can choose how to act. It is usually clear whether a particular action is good or bad. Muslims believe that if we deliberately choose to act against our consciences and do evil instead of good, then we must be prepared to pay the penalty.

The devil is always eager to gain control of a person's mind, so we need to be alert at all times. We must control our instincts. The path towards evil is always easy and tempting, and the path towards good may be hard and full of difficult decisions and sacrifices.

POINTLESS SUPERSTITION

God alone is the one who brings benefit. It is pointless and wrong to turn to anything else, such as lucky charms. These are superstitions (see unit 65).

DANGERS OF FATALISM

Fatalism is the belief that everything is unchangeable. It suggests that people are helpless and so weakens their sense of responsibility. Islam does not accept fatalism.

Muslims believe that God allows human beings to have minds that can reason and make choices. They say that our choices are not meaningless. Our future judgement will take account of the choices we have made. If there were no really free choices, there would be no need for Allah to send messengers or prophets.

> It is not poverty which I fear for you, but that you might come to desire the world as others before you desired it and it might destroy you as it destroyed them.
>
> (Hadith)

ALLAH'S RULES

- He doesn't test people beyond their strength to cope.
- Whoever does good or evil does it for the benefit or harm of their own soul.
- Allah does not force changes on people; He waits for them to change themselves.
- Everyone must bear their own burden.

FOR YOUR FOLDERS

1 Muslims do not believe that the world would be better if we did not have free will, despite the dangers of making wrong choices. Do you? Give reasons for your answer.

2 Obeying without question can be dangerous. Can you think of examples where this might be true?

THINKING POINTS

The Big Bang Theory says that the universe began to expand when a huge first atom exploded. Muslims ask:

- Where and what was this atom?
- How did it get there?
- Why did it explode?

THINGS TO DO

'The doctrine (teaching) of al-Qadr looks like belief in fate.' Do you agree? Give reasons for your answer.

Nothing happens that is not God's will

THE TEST

All Muslims believe in **akhirah**, that is, life after death. Human life is divided into two parts – each person has a life on earth, followed by eternal (everlasting) life. As earthly life is short by comparison to eternal life, then they believe that eternal life is more important.

Muslims believe life on earth has a very important purpose. It is a test. We may be born:

- wealthy or poor
- healthy or sick
- strong or weak
- beautiful or ugly
- generous or mean.

There is no point in moaning about our life. We don't know why things are the way they are, or what we are meant to learn. But to a Muslim, it is all God's will. We have free will to choose how we will react to the life we have been given.

WHAT IS IT THAT IS TESTED?

- Our characters – are we greedy, selfish, unkind, mean, spiteful or cowardly?
- Our reaction to misfortune – are we frightened, complaining, a burden to others?
- Our reaction to good fortune – are we selfish, conceited, arrogant, proud, miserly?
- Our way of life – are we dishonest, disrespectful, hurtful, unforgiving?

GOD KNOWS

A poor man owned nothing but a fine white stallion. One day he found the paddock empty. 'What terrible fortune!' said his friends. 'Maybe, maybe not,' he said.

Next day the stallion returned, bringing with him five beautiful wild mares. 'What wonderful fortune!' said his friends. 'Maybe, maybe not,' he said.

Next day his only son tried to tame a mare and was thrown. He broke his legs and became a cripple. 'What dreadful fortune!' said his friends. 'Maybe, maybe not.'

Then there was a war and all the young men went to fight in the army – all except the cripple. The army lost and all the young men were killed…

(a Muslim story)

THE RECORD

Muslims believe that:

- all people are responsible for their own future life
- how we respond to our tests is in our own hands and our actions earn our place in the next life
- what we do has a direct effect on ourselves alone
- our actions do not help or harm God; they only help or harm us
- our guardian angels know everything we do or think; they keep a record on which our judgement will be based
- God cannot be bought or bribed.

Every person's judgement is fastened round his neck; on the Day we will bring forth a book which shall be shown wide open. Read your book; you have no need of anyone but yourself to work out your account.

(surah 17:13–14)

JUDGEMENT

There is a time limit for everyone. Muslims believe that the test takes place in this earthly life and when it is over it will be too late to beg forgiveness from God.

After death comes judgement. Everyone stands alone before God and must answer for themselves. No one else's love or sorrow can free them from their sins.

God sent messengers to every generation to warn them and tell them what to do. If they chose to ignore the warnings and not do their best to behave well, then that was their choice and they must accept the outcome. Just as the people they hurt had to bear the consequences of their unkind actions in this life, they must accept the consequences of their actions in the next life.

To gain God's forgiveness a person must ask for it while there is still time, in this life. If a person refuses to repent and accept God's mercy, then hell is inevitable.

One burdened soul shall not bear the burden of another. And even if the heavy-laden [soul] should cry out for its burden [to be lifted] not one bit of it shall be carried, not even by the next of kin.

(surah 35:18)

It is the Day when one soul shall be powerless to plead for another.

(surah 82:19)

At evening, do not expect to live till morning; at morning, do not expect to live till evening. Take from your health for your illness, and from your life for your death.

(Hadith)

TALKING POINT

If God is all-powerful, He could interfere with the laws of nature to protect people from such things as floods, earthquakes and famines. So why doesn't He?

Brechin High School

FOR YOUR FOLDERS

1 How do Muslims believe you should react to good or bad fortune in this life?

2 What effect do Muslims believe your actions will have on the next (eternal) life?

3 Choose two passages from the Qur'an or Hadith. Write them out and explain what you think each one means.

FOR DISCUSSION

● It is harder to pass the test of life if one is born fortunate with little hardship to face.

● People who believe in God should accept everything without question and do nothing about it.

The companions of the right hand shall ask of the wretched, 'What has cast you into hell fire?' They will say, 'We were not of those who prayed, nor those who fed the poor, and we wasted our time with empty arguments, and we rejected…the Day of Reckoning – till we were forced to accept the Reality.'

(surah 74:39–47)

Muslims believe that they will not escape God's punishment on the Day of Judgement.

BELIEFS

- Humans are different from other animals because they know they are going to die.

- Death is not the end of existence.

- Even those who did not believe in God or life after death will have to accept it once they become aware of it.

- Unbelievers will beg for a second chance, to return to life and try again – but it will not be allowed.

BARZAKH

Muslims believe that when people die, Aszra'il, the angel of death, takes their souls to **barzakh**, which means 'barrier'. This is a state of waiting that comes between death and the Day of Judgement. It cannot be crossed by those who want to go back and warn others.

When death comes, one may say, 'O my Lord, send me back [to life] in order that I might put right the things I neglected [and did wrong].' By no means! This is no more than an excuse. Before them is a Barrier until the Day of Resurrection.

(surah 23:99–100)

THE END OF THE WORLD

The Qur'an describes the end of the world. There will be a blinding light, the sky will be split in two, the moon will disappear and the stars will be scattered. Mountains will be reduced to dust and the oceans will boil over with explosions of fire. The dead will be raised from their tombs and people will be asked what kept them from their God (see surahs 81 and 82).

THE REWARD

The reward will be paradise. The Qur'an describes it symbolically as a green garden, full of trees and flowers, and the sounds of water and birdsong.

In gardens of delight [they shall enjoy honour and happiness] facing each other on thrones: a cup will be passed to them from a clear-flowing fountain – delicious to drink…and beside them will be innocent women…

(surah 37:43–5)

THE PUNISHMENT

Hell, or **jahannam**, is also described symbolically. It is a horrible place of torment under the earth's crust. It is a place of fire, where the guilty will be forced to endure

Gardens of delight are the reward

burning winds, boiling water and black smoke (see surahs 14:16–17, 38:55–8).

Many people think the idea of God punishing people harshly does not go with the idea of His mercy. But no one will go to jahannam unless they refuse to accept God.

> I warn you of the flaming fire. None shall be cast into it but the most wretched, who has called the Truth a lie and turned his back.
>
> (surah 92:14–16)

THE AFTER-LIFE

All descriptions of the after-life are symbolic, because Muslims believe eternal life is lived in a different dimension. We shall be created in a new form beyond our imagining. Even marriage and family bonds may not continue, as individual souls outside time are not bound by the same relationships that exist in the world of time.

> When the trumpet is blown, there will be no relationships between them that day, nor will they ask after another.
>
> (surah 23:101)

> We have decreed Death to be in the midst of you, and We will not be prevented from changing your forms and creating you [again] in [forms] you know not.
>
> (surah 56:60–1)

Human beings, with their limited awareness, cannot understand the real nature of heaven and the presence of God, until the time comes.

> In Paradise, I prepare for the righteous believers what no eye has ever seen, no ear has ever heard, and what the deepest mind could never imagine.
>
> (Hadith, see also surah 32:17)

THINKING POINTS

- Does the idea of hell go against the Muslim idea of God's kindness and justice? Is God just if there are no punishments, only rewards?

- Is it possible that some people become so evil that they could never be forgiven?

- Does belief in life after death show weakness or strength of character?

- Does the burning fire mean there will be eternal punishment, or does it mean simply that evil will be 'burnt up' and cease to exist?

FOR YOUR FOLDERS

1 Explain these words and phrases.

   Day of Judgement; barzakh; jahannam

2 Do you think belief in a Day of Judgement would change:

   a the character of an individual

   b the way people treat each other

   c the way a Muslim practises their faith?

3 What do the surahs in this unit say about:

   a individual life after death

   b judgement?

4 The descriptions of paradise and hell are symbolic, not literal. Try to explain why the images are so powerful.

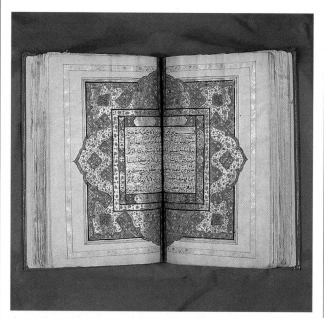

An eighteenth-century handwritten Qur'an from North India

SOME COMMANDMENTS

Here are some commandments from surah 17 of the Qur'an.

- Be kind to your parents, particularly in their old age.

- Do not commit adultery.

- Do not kill, except for just cause.

- Always keep your promises.

- In business and daily life be honest.

- Avoid gossip and slander.

- Do not take advantage of poor people or orphans.

(from surah 17)

SURAHS

There are 114 surahs, or chapters, in the Qur'an. All except one begin *'In the name of Allah, the Most Merciful, the Most Kind'*.

The surahs are not written in the order that Muhammad received them (see unit 16). The first surah, the **Fatihah** or 'opening' (see page 56) was not the first message revealed to the Prophet. The first revelation he received was the first part of surah 96, and the second was surah 74.

Each surah is named after some incident or word in it. Some have strange names, like the Spider, the Bee or the Cow.

THE EFFECT

The Qur'an was meant to be heard. Muslims believe that blessings flow from the sound of it. From the earliest times, people who heard and believed were greatly impressed. Many burst into tears, or would experience strong emotions. Some even fainted.

Muslims were taught to recite the Qur'an. Many men and women learned all the surahs by heart, and many still do. A person who does this is called a **hafiz** (plural **huffaz**). The Qur'an must still be learned in Arabic. When it is translated, some of the spirit or meaning is lost. Muslims do not treat translations with the same respect as the original.

THE QUR'AN COMPILED

After one battle in the early days of the persecution of Muslims, about 70 huffaz died. Abu Bakr was worried about maintaining the accuracy of the recitations after the Prophet's death. So Abu Bakr asked the Prophet's secretary, **Zaid ibn Thabit**, to make a special book of all the revelations, in the order the Prophet had taught him. Zaid, who was himself a hafiz, wrote down exactly what he had memorized. He accepted that every word was the word of God, just as Muslims believe it today. It was completed during the Prophet's lifetime. It was guarded by **Hafsah**, daughter of Umar and one of the Prophet's wives.

To ensure that only true readings were learned, copies of Hafsah's book were sent to the chief places as the standard text. Two of these copies still exist, one in Istanbul (Turkey) and one in Tashkent (Uzbekistan).

The Qur'an is always treated with respect

THE QUR'AN HONOURED

Muslims treat the Qur'an with great respect. While it is being read:

- you must not speak or make a noise
- you must not eat or drink
- you must not touch it unnecessarily.

Before reading or touching it:

- you must wash carefully, or take a bath
- you must be in the right frame of mind
- women must not be having a period.

When not in use, it should be placed high up, with nothing put on top of it except its cover. It must be kept free from dust.

It is never allowed to touch the ground and may be placed on a **kursi**, a special stool, for reading. The art of **calligraphy** (beautiful writing) was developed because it was an honour to copy the Qur'an and it had to be done as beautifully as possible.

THINGS TO DO

1 If possible, listen to a recording of the Qur'an being recited. You may find it on a CD-ROM. Try to listen alone for a few minutes. Write down your impressions.

2 Make a decorative card or poster, using the laws of surah 17.

3 Explain why Muslims believe the Tashkent Qur'an (and all others) contains the exact words revealed to the Prophet.

Brechin High School

QUICK QUIZ

1 What is a hafiz?

2 What is a kursi used for?

3 Why is calligraphy important to a Muslim?

4 Who compiled the Qur'an in writing?

5 Which woman kept the book?

6 Where could you now find an original copy?

7 What must you do before reading the Qur'an?

FOR YOUR FOLDERS

In what ways do Muslims show their deep respect for the Qur'an? (Mention behaviour and how they take care of the book.)

He is not a believer who eats his fill while his neighbour is hungry.

The warrior who truly fights for God's cause is he who looks after a widow or a poor person.

If you think of God, you will find Him there before you.

(Hadiths)

Hadiths are the recorded words, actions and instructions of the Prophet. They are often called 'traditions'. After Muhammad's death, many of these collections of reports about him appeared. They are greatly respected by Muslims, but are completely separate from the Qur'an.

There are two sorts of Hadiths.

- *Prophetic Hadiths* are the words and teachings of the Prophet himself. His sayings show that he was a man of great wisdom and kindness and a true servant of God.

- *Sacred Hadiths*, or **Hadith Qudsi**, are called this because Muslims believe they were revealed directly to the Prophet by God. They are not part of the Qur'an, but Muslims regard them with great respect.

SOURCES

The two main and most reliable collections of Hadiths were those made by the early scholars Muhammad ibn Isma'il al-Bukhari, who listed 2762 traditions, and Abul Husayn Muslim ibn al-Hajjaj, who listed another 4000.

The earliest accounts of the life of the Prophet were written by men who knew the Prophet's studious wife, Aishah. When Muslims need help with a problem, especially in today's complicated society, if there is no clear answer in the Qur'an, they turn to the Hadiths for guidance.

THE CHAINS

In order to find out how reliable a particular Hadith is, Muslims trace them back to the original source. Each saying is transmitted (passed down) through a chain of teachers. The most famous transmitters of Hadiths were the Prophet's wives Aishah and Umm Salamah, and his close companions.

HADITH QUDSI

Hadith Qudsi were messages from God that the Prophet received as revelations or in dreams, then he explained them using his own words. That is, the meaning was from God, but the words are the Prophet's own.

The Sacred Hadiths are mainly about belief, worship and conduct, and not the more practical aspects of everyday living. They have a distinct style, either commands direct from Allah to His servants, or through conversations with them.

INTERPRETATIONS

If a Hadith does not seem to fit the general principles of Islam, or contradicts the Qur'an, then the memory or understanding of the transmitter could be at fault.

Scholars study the chain of transmission carefully to make sure that a Hadith is reliable.

The companions of the Prophet were especially careful to check the Hadiths and would not preach them unless they were very sure that they were his words.

SELECTION OF HADITHS QUDSI

I am with him when he makes mention of Me. If he draws near to Me a hand's span, I draw near to him an arm's length.

On the Day of Judgement Allah will say: 'O son of Adam, I fell ill and you did not visit Me.' The man will answer, 'O Lord, how could I have visited You when You are Lord of the Worlds?' He will say – 'Did you not know that My servant had fallen ill, and you did not visit him? Did you not know that if you had visited him, you would have found Me with him?'

A man said of another – 'By Allah, Allah will never forgive him!' At this Allah the Almighty said – 'Who is this who swears by Me that I will never forgive a certain person? Truly, I have forgiven him already.'

If he has in his heart goodness to the weight of one barley corn, and has said There is no God but Me, he shall come out of hell-fire.

(from Ezzedin Ibrahim *et al.* (eds) *Forty Hadith Qudsi*, Dar al-Qur'an al-Kareem, Beirut, 1980)

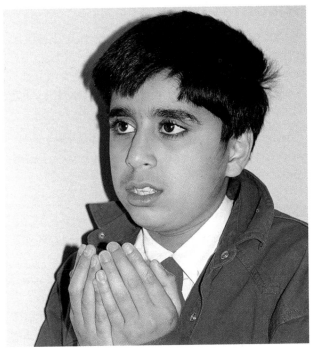

'If you think of God, you will find Him there before you' (Hadith)

THINGS TO DO

Choose two or three Hadiths in this unit. Write them out carefully on a decorated page.
Or
Use a 'script' style font and decorative border from your PC to carry out this task.

FOR YOUR FOLDERS

1 Explain the meaning of the word 'Hadith'. What is the difference between Prophetic Hadiths and Hadiths Qudsi?

2 How do Muslim scholars decide whether Hadiths are reliable?

THINKING POINTS

- Some Muslims regard the Hadiths as vital information for guidance in life. Others are more cautious. Why is this so?

- Muslims give Allah the titles 'the Compassionate', 'the Merciful'. How do the Hadith Qudsi on this page bear this out?

NOBODY IS PERFECT!

Worship is based on the feeling that there is a higher standard that we should all be trying to reach. People who believe in God feel that this belief changes the way they live. They are trying to be better people.

Turning to God in respect, submission and wonder is called **Ibadah**, from the word **abd** meaning 'servant' or 'slave'.

WHY WORSHIP?

It is difficult to explain the need that some people have to worship. It is like trying to explain why a certain thing is beautiful. You may see beauty and be lost in wonder and admiration of it. Another person may not see it at all. It is the same with awareness of God.

THE FAILINGS

Muslims believe that worship has to be pure, and free from three 'sins':

- **kufr** – disbelief, ingratitude: this may be choosing to deny that God exists, or not caring whether He exists or not; it is when people feel no sense of responsibility and no purpose in life

- **shirk** – 'association' (see unit 12): having wrong ideas about God: comparing Him with other beings, or believing that some other being shares His power and can judge or forgive sins

- **tughyan** – arrogance, tyranny: when people become over-religious and make other people feel small or stupid, or when they become fanatical or try to force others to accept their own rules or opinions, which is against the Law of God.

◇

Turning to God in prayer

TRUE WORSHIP

For Muslims, ibadah (worship) is a way of life, involving:

- **iman** – belief
- **amal** – action
- **ihsan** – realization.

No one can *make* ihsan happen. It is when faith enters a person's heart, and they feel full of love and gratitude towards God. Religious teachers may lead people towards God, but a person cannot be made to feel faith. It is a matter of 'awareness'.

The Prophet described ihsan like this.

> Ihsan is to worship Allah as if you are seeing Him; for He sees you, even if you do not see Him.

(Hadith)

Muslims believe that God created us. We belong to God and must return to Him and give an account of ourselves. Submission to God means making your attitudes and behaviour conform to His will. It affects a person's whole life. Musims call this **din**.

Any action that a person makes to please God is worship. For Muslims, this covers everything – going to school or work, eating and drinking, enjoying the pleasures of life, every part of our behaviour. Muslims aim to:

- reform their lives
- develop dignity
- develop patience and courage in the face of hardship
- enjoy and appreciate God's gifts to the full
- strive to be good and defeat evil.

> God does not accept beliefs if they are not expressed in deeds; and your deeds are worthless if they do not back up your beliefs.
>
> (Hadith)

Some Muslims believe they sometimes may have to fight and even die for their beliefs. This is an act of worship or 'witness'.

JIHAD

Someone who dies for the faith is called a **shahid** or martyr. Fighting a war for the sake of God is called **jihad**.

Jihad actually means 'striving'. It means being ready to give up everything, even your life, for the sake of Allah. But the real meaning of jihad is trying your best to live correctly and working as hard as possible to see God's rules being obeyed in society.

> Those who do not believe take their comfort in this life, and eat as cattle eat; fire will be their future abode.
>
> (surah 47:12)

INTENTION

People are not all saints, and many often fall short or fail completely in their aim in life. But Muslims believe that God judges us by our intentions, or **niyyah**, and is merciful even when we do not succeed. However, our intentions should be honest and we should make as much effort as possible.

TALKING POINTS

- Faith and actions are important for a Muslim. Which is worth more, in your opinion? Give reasons for your answer.
- There are many examples of tughyan – people who believe in God but behave like tyrants. Write down the names of some examples.

THINGS TO DO

Make a poster with the theme 'Every action that pleases God is an act of worship'. (You can use your PC for this task.)

FOR YOUR FOLDERS

1 Does belief in God really change a person's life? Give reasons for your answer.
2 Explain what iman, amal and ihsan mean in Muslim worship.
3 Explain the words kufr, shirk, jihad and niyyah.

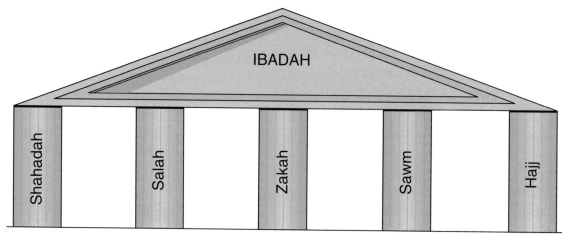

IBADAH

Shahadah | Salah | Zakah | Sawm | Hajj

The five pillars of Islam

PILLARS

Muslims think of their faith as a kind of temple for God held up by five pillars. These are the five basic duties for all Muslims.

- **Shahadah** – bearing witness: the declaration of faith that there is truly one God and that Muhammad was His messenger or Prophet
- **Salah** – prayer five times a day
- **Zakah** – charity, giving money for the poor
- **Sawm** – fasting during the month of Ramadan
- **Hajj** – making the pilgrimage to Makkah.

These pillars do not include the whole of Islam, but they are the foundations of Islam. If one of the pillars is weak, the whole 'building' suffers.

SHAHADAH

This is the first pillar of Islam. The creed (statement of belief) of Islam is short and simple:

> Ashadu an la ilaha il-allahu wa Muhammadar rasulullah.

> I believe there is no God but Allah, and Muhammad is the Messenger of God.

Muslims repeat the shahadah first thing on waking and last thing before they go to sleep. They are the first words whispered into the ears of a new-born baby and, if possible, the last words spoken to the dying.

The longer creed is the Iman-I-Mufassal, the 'faith in detail':

> I believe in Allah,
> in His angels,
> in His revealed Books,
> in all of His prophets,
> in the Day of Judgement,
> in that everything – both good and bad– comes from Him, and
> in life after death.

THE SACRIFICE

Bearing witness is more than mere words. Being a witness involves your whole life. Muslims lay down their lives as a sacrifice to God. Life is precious, but if you are shahid (ready to die for your faith) you know that your life does not belong to you, but to God.

THE CALL TO PRAYER

Muhammad established the **adhan** or call to prayer in 623 CE after he arrived in Madinah. They are the words with which Bilal, the freed slave, first called the faithful to prayer.

*The **Mu'adhin** (Muezzin) calls the faithful to prayer*

THE MUSLIM CALL TO PRAYER

The English form of the Muslim call to prayer or adhan is:

God is Great (said four times)
I bear witness that there is no God but God (twice)
I bear witness that Muhammad is the Prophet of God (twice)
Come to prayer! (twice)
Come to success! (twice)
God is Great! (twice)
There is no God but God' (once)
At dawn prayers, this phrase is added:
Prayer is better than sleep! (twice)

FOR DISCUSSION

- Should Muslims living in a non-Muslim community make their religion obvious or keep it private?
- Should there be prayer-rooms for Muslims in schools and public buildings?

Brechin High School

THINGS TO DO

1 Try to listen to a recording of the call to prayer (there may be one on CD-ROM). Make notes of your reaction to its sound.

2 Survey your local area for signs of Muslim commitment, e.g. mosques, special shops, people in Muslim dress (prayer caps, women wearing scarves, long coats, etc.).

FOR YOUR FOLDERS

1 Make a list of the seven sections of the Iman-I-Mufassal. Present these as a diagram (perhaps a flower with six petals) with 'I believe in Allah' at the centre.

2 Do you think it takes courage to make a public declaration of faith? Explain your answer.

Wash hands three times

Snuff water into nostrils

Wash face three times

Wash arms to elbows three times

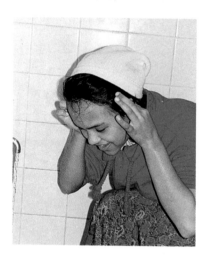

Wash head, ears and back of neck

Wash feet to ankles three times

THE DISCIPLINE

It is not easy in the modern world to live life as a witness for God. Muslims believe they must make a deliberate, conscious effort that is trained and disciplined.

THE MEANING

Of course, people can pray to God at any time and in any place. But a Muslim performs salah, a special kind of prayer, five times a day.

During salah, Muslims put everything else out of their minds to concentrate on God, praising Him, thanking Him and asking for His forgiveness and blessing. Salah is a duty that must be performed at work, at home, when travelling, or even at war. If Muslims are too old or ill to stand or kneel, they can go through the motions in their hearts while sitting or lying down.

Muslim children begin to practise salah when they are about seven; by the age of ten they are expected to do it as a duty.

PREPARATION

- The place for prayer must be clean (a special mat is often used).

- The mind should be attentive. The body and clothes must be clean.

- A man's clothes should cover his body from the navel to the knees.

- A woman's entire body should be covered, except for face and hands.
- A woman should not be wearing make-up or perfume.
- Prayer begins with the ritual wash, or **wudu**.

WUDU

Wudu is part of the discipline and preparation for prayer. Most Muslims do not wash just because they are dirty. Some Muslims may even take a complete bath (called **ghusl**), but most go through the pattern set out below. (See also the pictures opposite.)

1 Declaration of intent (niyyah). They must focus all their attention on God.
2 Wash the hands up to the wrists three times.
3 Rinse the mouth three times.
4 Snuff water into the nostrils and blow out three times.
5 Wash the face three times.
6 Wash the arms up to the elbows three times.
7 Pass wet hands over the top of the head and round the back of the neck. Wipe out the ears with the index finger, and the back of the neck with the thumbs.
8 Wash the feet up to the ankles three times. (See surah 5:6.)

In the desert, if no water is available, then a symbolic wash, called **tayammum**, can be performed using clean sand.

QIBLAH

After the preparation, Muslims stand on a prayer mat or alongside other Muslims in an orderly fashion at the mosque. They face Makkah. The direction of Makkah is called **qiblah**. In a mosque there is a special alcove, called a **mihrab**, in the qiblah wall. If they are not in a mosque, some Muslims use a small compass to show the direction of Makkah.

QUICK QUIZ

Explain the meaning of these words.

1 wudu   4 tayammum
2 qiblah   5 mihrab
3 niyyah

FOR YOUR FOLDERS

1 Muslims believe that a person can pray to God at any time and in any place. Why do you think they go to such trouble for salah?

2 Briefly describe the preparations a Muslim has to make before they perform salah.

3 Which part of the washing do you think takes most effort? Why is this?

THINKING POINT

How do you think praying at regular times affects someone's thoughts and activities during a normal day? How difficult is this for Muslims in non-Muslim schools?

THINGS TO DO

1 Draw a series of diagrams to illustrate wudu. (You can use pin-people.)

2 Explain how salah is different from 'spur of the moment' prayers.

3 Make a list of some of the everyday things that might stop a person thinking of God.

THE AIMS OF SALAH

The aims of salah are:

- to bring people close to Allah
- to unite body and soul in worship
- to keep them from indecent, shameful and forbidden activities
- to calm down dangerous feelings and control baser instincts
- to bring a sense of peace and tranquillity
- to show equality, unity and brotherhood
- to develop patience, courage, hope and confidence
- to develop gratitude and humility
- to demonstrate obedience
- to train in cleanliness, purity and punctuality
- to develop discipline and will-power
- to remind people constantly of God and His greatness
- to draw the mind away from personal problems and focus them on God – who could at any moment change the course of a person's life.

TIMES

The five times for salah are:

- salut-ul-fajr – just before sunrise
- salut-ul-zuhr – early afternoon
- salat-ul-asr – between mid-afternoon and sunset
- salat-ul-maghrib – in the evening, after sunset but before dark
- salat-ul-isha – between darkness and dawn.

Muslims do not say salah at sunrise, noon or sunset as these times were used by pagan sun-worshippers.

CONGREGATION

Muslims may pray at home, but prefer to pray together if they can. In Muslim countries it is not unusual to see Muslims praying in the street or wherever they happen to be when the call to prayer is sounded. When they pray together, they stand shoulder to shoulder in a line, facing the Ka'bah shrine in Makkah.

Muslims praying in the street

PRAYER START TIMES

Islamic month	Day	Calendar date	Sehri ends – Fajr starts	Sun rise	Zuhr	Asr	Sunset Maghrib	Isha
21 Muhrm	**Fri**	**1st July**	**2.55**	**4.35**	**2.56**	**6.47**	**9.40**	**11.00**
22 Muhrm	Sat	2nd July	2.55	4.35	1.15	6.47	9.40	11.00
23 Muhrm	Sun	3rd July	2.56	4.36	1.15	6.47	9.39	10.59
24 Muhrm	Mon	4th July	2.57	4.37	1.16	6.47	9.39	10.59
25 Muhrm	Tue	5th July	2.58	4.38	1.16	6.46	9.38	10.58
26 Muhrm	Wed	6th July	2.59	4.39	1.16	6.46	9.38	10.58
27 Muhrm	Thu	7th July	3.00	4.40	1.16	6.46	9.37	10.57
28 Muhrm	**Fri**	**8th July**	**3.01**	**4.41**	**1.16**	**6.46**	**9.36**	**10.56**
29 Muhrm	Sat	9th July	3.02	4.42	1.16	6.45	9.35	10.55
30 Muhrm	Sun	10th July	3.03	4.43	1.17	6.45	9.35	10.55
1 Safar	Mon	11th July	3.04	4.44	1.17	6.45	9.34	10.54
2 Safar	Tue	12th July	3.05	4.45	1.17	6.44	9.33	10.53
3 Safar	Wed	13th July	3.06	4.46	1.17	6.44	9.32	10.52
4 Safar	Thu	14th July	3.08	4.48	1.17	6.43	9.31	10.51

Prayer times for two weeks in July, Hull

PRAYER MATS

Muslims do not have to use mats for prayer. They are meant to make sure there is a clean space to kneel on. Muslims prayer mats are quite distinctive. They may have geometric patterns or pictures of famous mosques. They never have pictures of living things, or images of God, angels or the Prophets. When not in use they are folded or rolled up. They are not used to cover floors, as fireside rugs or general room decorations.

Muslims can pray at home

FOR YOUR FOLDERS

1 What are the main aims of salah?

2 Why are prayers not said at sunrise, sunset or noon?

THINKING POINTS

- Do you think it is important to have a place set aside specially for prayers to God? Give reasons for your answer.

- What would you be doing at the Muslim prayer times?

THINGS TO DO

1 Explain why prayer mats are used.

2 What sort of decorations are allowed to be used on prayer mats?

3 Design a prayer mat. Remember not to use animals or humans in your design. Look at some designs in books in the library, or on a CD-ROM to give you ideas.

بِسْمِ اللهِ الرَّحْمٰنِ الرَّحِيْمِ ۝
اَلْحَمْدُ لِلّٰهِ رَبِّ الْعٰلَمِيْنَ ۝ الرَّحْمٰنِ الرَّحِيْمِ ۝ مٰلِكِ يَوْمِ الدِّيْنِ ۝
اِيَّاكَ نَعْبُدُ وَاِيَّاكَ نَسْتَعِيْنُ ۝ اِهْدِنَا الصِّرَاطَ الْمُسْتَقِيْمَ ۝
صِرَاطَ الَّذِيْنَ اَنْعَمْتَ عَلَيْهِمْ غَيْرِ الْمَغْضُوْبِ عَلَيْهِمْ
وَلَا الضَّآلِّيْنَ ۝

THE FATIHAH

The Fatihah, or opening, is the first surah of the Qur'an. It is recited at every salah. The English form is:

In the name of Allah, the Compassionate, the Merciful.
All praise be to Allah,
the Lord of all the worlds,
The Most Merciful, the Most Kind,
Master of the Day of Judgement.
You alone do we worship,
From You alone do we seek help.
Show us the [next step along] the straight path
of those earning Your favour.
Keep us from the path of those earning Your anger,
those who are going astray.

THE RAK'AHS

The **rak'ahs** are a set of movements that follow a fixed pattern and accompany salah. The movements are not as important as the intention of the worshipper.

Woe to those who pray, but are unmindful of their prayer, or pray only to be seen by people.

(surah 107:4–6)

When a person is drowsy during prayers, let him sleep until he knows what he recites.

(Hadith)

Muslims may carry out as many rak'ahs as they like at each salah, but the compulsory ones are:

- salat-ul-fajr – two rak'ahs
- salat-ul-zuhr – four rak'ahs
- salat-ul-asr – four rak'ahs
- salat-ul-maghrib – three rak'ahs
- salat-ul-isha – four rak'ahs.

There are eight separate actions in each rak'ah.

1 **Takbir** – shutting out the world and concentrating only on God. Muslims stand to attention with hands raised level with their shoulders, and say:

'Allahu Akbar' – 'Allah is the Most Great'

2 They place the right hand over the left on the chest and say:

'Glory and praise to Thee, O God; blessed is Thy name and exalted is Thy majesty. There is no God other than Thee. I come, seeking shelter from Satan, the rejected one.'

Next, they recite Fatihah, followed by any other passage from the Qur'an, e.g.

He is God, the One; He is the Eternal Absolute; none is born of Him, and neither is He born. There is none like unto Him.

(surah 112)

The Prophet said that passages for public prayer should be short. He told off **imams** who demanded too much (see unit 69).

3 Ruku – Muslims bow, placing their hands on their knees. This shows they respect as well as love God. They repeat three times:

'Glory be to my Great Lord,
and praise be to Him.'

4 Qiyam – they stand up again and say:

'God always hears those who praise Him.
O God, all praise be to Thee,
O God greater than all else.'

5 The humblest position is called **sujud**. Muslims kneel, touching the ground with their forehead, nose, palms of both hands, knees and toes, and say three times:

'Glory be to my Lord, the Most High.
God is greater than all else.'

6 They kneel again, taking a moment's rest before the next prostration. They say three times:

'O my Master, forgive me.'

7 Sujud is repeated once more.

8 Muslims either repeat the rak'ah or finish. The last action is to turn their heads to right and left to acknowledge the other worshippers and their guardian angels, with the words of the **salam**:

'Peace be with you, and the mercy of Allah.'

The prayer said in Madinah is worth thousands of others, except that in Makkah, which is worth a hundred thousand. But worth more than all this is the prayer said in the house where no one sees but God…

(Hadith)

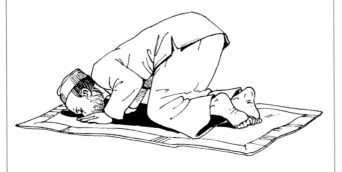

Being humble before God

FOR YOUR FOLDERS

1 Do you think the physical movements of the rak'ahs make any difference to the way a Muslim feels about prayer?

2 Read the Hadith on page 56. Try to explain what you think this is saying about private, personal prayer.

THINGS TO DO

Copy out this list of feelings. Tick the ones that you think Muslims feel when they pray (you may need to use a dictionary to help you).

conceit
humility
pride
forgiveness
devotion
sense of togetherness
embarrassment
superiority
love
desire to be forgiven
desire to show off
putting God before self

An imam gives a sermon at Friday prayers

On Fridays Muslim men meet together in a special congregation (called **jamaah**) for the midday prayer. The word for Friday is **jumu'ah**, so sometimes these 'communal prayers' are called salat-ul-jumu'ah. They try to meet at the mosque or in a room set aside for worship. In Muslim countries all shops and businesses close for the midday hour on Fridays.

> O ye who believe! When the call is heard for the prayer of the day of congregation, leave your trading and hasten to remember Allah!
>
> (surah 62.9)

CONCENTRATION

When Muslims say their prayers they:

- should not talk or look around
- should not make any movement or noise that might draw attention to themselves or distract others
- should not try to look too holy – this might suggest pride and conceit
- should concentrate on the prayer and focus their minds only on this.

Friday prayers consist of two rak'ahs. People then say a private prayer and return to work.

KHUTBAH

Before Friday prayers, the teacher or imam gives two **khutbah** (sermon or talk) based on verses from the Qur'an or the traditions about Muhammad. Or they may talk about subjects of topical interest. Sometimes the sermons are political, especially in times of social and political unrest.

Islam does not have paid priests or religious leaders. The imam can be any Muslim man of good character who has:

- good knowledge of the faith
- gained the respect of his fellow Muslims
- studied the Qur'an and Hadiths
- a reputation for piety and common sense.

Some mosques do not have full-time imams, so their teacher may have a paid job outside the mosque.

WOMEN

Women usually pray at home, but when they pray at the mosque they form rows behind the men. They do not sit among the men for worship. This is so that men and women can concentrate on their prayers and not be distracted by thoughts about the opposite sex, or worries about family matters.

Shutting out the world and concentrating on God

Reciting al-Fatihah

Bowing from the waist

Prostration before Allah

Kneeling with palms of hands on knees

Salam – greeting the angels at the end of prayer

FOR YOUR FOLDERS

1 Use the pictures above and the information in unit 27 to draw a series of pin-people showing the prayer positions.

2 What are the qualities needed for an imam?

3 Do you think it is good or bad for a community to choose its own imam? Give reasons for your answer.

FOR DISCUSSION

- How important do you think it is for members of a religion to meet together regularly for worship?

- Why do Muslims think it is best for women to pray separately at the back of the group?

Private du'a prayer

DU'A

People who love God and feel close to Him pray many times during the day. Muslims believe their whole lives are controlled by God, but they still feel it is natural to want to speak to Him, tell Him about their worries and ask for help and guidance in times of anxiety or suffering.

These personal supplications or requests, are called **du'a** prayers. They may be:

- thanking God for some blessing received (e.g. recovery from illness, birth of a child)

- asking for help

- asking for forgiveness

- general requests for God's guidance and blessing.

TALKING POINTS

- If people believe that God is all-knowing, and knows what you need before you ask, is there any point in private prayer?

- Do private prayers suggest a lack of faith in God? Give reasons for your answer.

FOR DISCUSSION

Muslim women pray both salah and du'a at home instead of going to the mosque. Some homes have a whole room set aside for worship. Many Muslim women take their religion very seriously, and do not find the rules about modest clothing and removal of tights for foot-washing a burden.

What effects do you think that praying in the home have on

a the atmosphere within the home

and

b the behaviour and attitude of a Muslim housewife during her normal working day?

SUBHA

Some Muslims use a string of 99 beads, called a **subha**, as an aid to prayer. They pass the beads through their fingers as they praise God, saying 'Glory be to Allah', 'Thanks be to Allah' and 'God is great' 33 times each.

Muslims try to make God their first thought on waking, and their last before sleeping. They often think of Him during the day. This is also du'a.

Praising God using the subha

PERSONAL PRAYER

Any prayer for yourself, for your family, for the solution to a problem, or for protection, is du'a.

Muslims believe the best du'a prayer is not to ask God to take away the problem, but to ask for strength and faith to endure the test.

> O Allah, I have been unjust to myself and no one grants pardon for sins except You. Forgive me, therefore, in Your compassion, for surely You are the Forgiver, the Merciful.
>
> (du'a prayer)

In the name of Allah, the Most
   Merciful, the Most Kind.
I seek refuge in the Lord of the
   Daybreak
from the evil of what He has created;
from the evil of the intense darkness;
from the evil of those who practise
   secret arts;
from the evil of the envious one.

(surah 113)

Brechin High School

Giving zakah at Regent's Park mosque

GIVING

All Muslims are expected to be generous and kind. When they give as an act of charity, which means kindness, they do not expect to be rewarded for it. They may give to famine appeals, for example. This kind of giving is called **sadaqah**.

Zakah is another kind of giving. Muslims pay 2.5 per cent (one-fortieth) of their savings on a regular basis as a duty. Zakah means 'to cleanse'. When Muslims pay zakah it stops them from desiring things or being greedy. The 2.5 percentage applies to cash, bank savings and jewellery.

> Be steadfast in prayer and regular in giving. Whatever good you send forth from your souls before you, you will find [again] with God; for God sees well all that you do.
>
> (surah 2:110, 270)

AIMS

The aim of paying zakah is to control greed and selfishness. Muslims believe that zakah cleanses their hearts from love of money and the desire to hold on to it. They believe that money should be used for promoting goodness and justice in the world.

Zakah money may only be used:

- to help the poor
- to clear debts
- to help needy travellers
- to free captives
- to win people over to the cause of Allah
- to pay those who collect it.

The idea behind Zakah is based on social welfare and the fair distribution of wealth. The Qur'an forbids Muslims to charge interest (called usury) on money. (See surah 2:275, 278. See also unit 59.)

> He is not a believer who eats his fill while his neighbour remains hungry by his side.
>
> (Hadith)

Zakah is usually paid in secret so that rich people are not seen to be showing off and poor people do not feel ashamed to receive (surah 2:271). However, Muslims may sometimes be encouraged to give openly, to persuade others to give.

Muslims believe that when you give for God's sake, you must do so willingly.

> O believers! Don't cancel your charity by reminders of your generosity, or by holding it against them – like those who give their wealth only to be seen by others...They are like hard, barren rock on which is little soil. Heavy rain falls on it and leaves it just a bare stone.
>
> (surah 2:264)

RATES OF ZAKAH

Wealth	Amount	Rate
Cash in hand or bank	Over value of 595g silver	2.5%
Gold and silver	85g gold, 595g silver	2.5%
Trading goods	Value of 595g silver	2.5%
Cows and buffaloes	30	1
Goats and sheep	40	1
Mining produce	Any	20%
Agricultural	Per harvest	10% from rain-watered land
		5% from irrigated land
Camels	Per 5	1 sheep or goat

GOD IS THE OWNER

Muslims believe they have a duty to help those who cannot earn their own living, or earn so little that it does not cover basic needs. Muslims feel the poor have a claim on the rich.

Muslims believe that:

- people do not *own* anything – God lends them what they have in trust. So anything that is given for God is going back to its rightful owner

- God chooses who to make rich or poor – the rich are obliged to give to the poor

- everyone is born naked and will die naked, so there is no point clinging to possessions or letting them rule you.

TALKING POINTS

- A person who gives money away is richer than a person who keeps it.

- The most valuable things in life cannot be bought with money.

- Governments should help the poor.

THINGS TO DO

1 Working in a group, create a collage of different newspaper pictures illustrating world poverty. Give it a title, such as 'We are one family'.

2 Make a list of the things that are more valuable than money.

FOR YOUR FOLDERS

1 How does giving zakah help a Muslim to become less selfish and less attached to possessions?

2 Do you think zakah is a reasonable amount of a person's wealth to devote to God? Give reasons for your answer.

QUICK QUIZ

1 Explain the difference between zakah and sadaqah.

2 What is the zakah rate for cash savings?

3 What are the zakah rates for cows, sheep, camels, coal and oil?

O believers, you must fast so that you may learn self-restraint.

(surah 2:183)

To fast means to go without food for a certain time, usually for a religious reason. During the 29–30 days of Ramadan healthy adult Muslims go without all the pleasures of the body, including eating and drinking, during the hours of daylight. This is called sawm and is an act of self-control.

From dawn to dusk, nothing must pass the lips, not even chewing-gum or a drink. Muslims must try very hard to avoid bad thoughts or actions. If the thoughts or actions are wrong, then the fast means nothing.

> If you do not give up telling lies God will have no need of your giving up food and drink.

> There are many who fast during the day and pray all night, but they gain nothing but hunger and sleeplessness.

(Hadith)

AIMS OF SAWM

Sawm is intended to help Muslims to:

- develop self-control
- overcome selfishness, greed and laziness
- control their passions and appetite
- prepare for suffering that may happen later
- experience the pain of hunger, and so develop sympathy for the poor
- gain spiritual strength
- share hardship with other Muslims.

After a few hours of lack of food and drink the body begins to feel uncomfortable. But Muslims let the mind control the body. It gradually becomes easier to resist temptation.

Of course, a Muslim could cheat. But that would be pointless because the fast is a matter between the believer and God alone.

THOSE EXCUSED FASTING

The following people do not have to fast:

- children under twelve
- pregnant and nursing mothers
- the aged
- those who are sick, or making a journey.

If possible, a Muslim who misses days of fasting can make them up later.

RAMADAN

Ramadan is the ninth month of the Muslim year. This was the month when Muhammad received the first message from God (see units 3 and 37).

The Muslim calendar is based on the moon. Ramadan falls eleven days earlier each year. When it falls in the summer, the days of fasting can be very long.

Muslims are excited as they wait for the new moon to appear at the start of Ramadan. It may be announced on the radio. Sometimes a cannon is fired or there is some other public signal.

THE NIGHT MEALS

Each night there is more excitement as a day of fasting has been completed and Muslims feel a great sense of achievement. Believers break the fast with a small snack. A bigger meal follows later. An early meal can be taken before sunrise.

Ramadan ends with the feast of **Id-ul-Fitr** (see unit 38).

Breaking the fast

THOUGHTS OF A FIRST TIME FASTER

Although the fast was only for 30 days out of 365 it seemed like a lifetime!

I had to go without food and drink all day, but the hardest part was going without my 11 a.m. coffee and cigarette! By 3 p.m. I was in agony, but by 6 p.m. when I had to feed my non-Muslim family, I was really past eating. I actually felt a bit sick.

I got a bit bad-tempered and sometimes I had to lie down in the afternoon. It made me realize how hard it is for Muslims who go out to work.

It was rather nice to see other Muslims across the street and know that we had a kind of secret, and that passers-by had no idea what we were up to.

FOR YOUR FOLDERS

1 In what ways are Muslims drawn together by the fast of Ramadan?

2 Why might a person's fast be of no value?

THINGS TO DO

1 Imagine you are a Muslim. Write a letter to a friend explaining about Ramadan, and how it might affect your behaviour at school.

2 Try to fast for a school day. Keep a log of your feelings during the day. You could make this a sponsored class event. (Don't be silly about it – if you feel faint, have a drink or something to eat.)

QUICK QUIZ

1 What does it mean to fast?

2 What are the aims of fasting for Muslims?

3 Which is the Muslim month for fasting?

4 Which people are excused from fasting?

5 What is the name of the feast that ends Ramadan?

The Ka'bah, Makkah

GOING ON HAJJ

A pilgrimage is a special journey to visit a place of religious importance. Every Muslim hopes to perform the Hajj, or pilgrimage to Makkah. The Hajj is a duty for all Muslims to visit the Ka'bah and stand before God on Mount **Arafat** at least once in their lifetime.

Some people save up all their lives to be able to go. Sometimes a family or community will club together to send one representative.

The true Hajj has to be made between 8 and 13 Dhul-Hijjah (the twelfth month). A pilgrimage made at any other time does not have the same importance.

For Muslims, Hajj is a complete break from everyday life, as the pilgrim fixes his whole attention on God.

CONDITIONS

The rules for pilgrims are that they must be:

- Muslim – non-Muslims are not allowed in Makkah: it is not a tourist attraction

- of sound mind and able to understand the importance of the event

- physically fit and able to undertake the strain of the journey

- able to provide for dependants they leave behind

- able to pay for the Hajj without having to obtain the money dishonestly.

In the past it took months or even years to get to Makkah and back. Today pilgrims can fly to the Hajj Terminal at Jeddah airport. Pilgrims come from a wide social and racial mix, and all feel united in their pilgrimage.

NIYYAH

If Muslims cannot go on Hajj because of ill health or because they cannot afford it, then it is the niyyah, or intention (see unit 23) that counts.

Muslims can join the pilgrims in spirit and in prayer. They can pay for someone else, who has already done their own Hajj, to go on their behalf. Or they can give their Hajj savings to charity.

Today the Saudi Arabian Government gives about 300 million dollars a year to the Ministry of Pilgrimage and over a million people gather on Hajj. The Hajj Terminal at King Abdul Aziz Airport in Jeddah can take ten jumbo jets at a time.

People are appointed to help pilgrims and plan their visit and their accommodation. It is very difficult having so many visitors at once. People may get split up, lost, or overcome by heat and exhaustion. But Muslims have a wonderful feeling of being one great family. The joy of being a pilgrim shuts out all other difficulties and problems.

FOR YOUR FOLDERS

1 How could Muslims take part in Hajj, even if they could not go?

2 Why is the niyyah, or intention, to do Hajj as important as the pilgrimage itself?

3 Muslims may take great pride in the title 'Hajji' or 'Hajjah' (a Muslim who has completed Hajj). Why do you think this is?

4 Write a list of the conditions for pilgrims on Hajj. Why do you think these conditions were made?

The camp site in the valley of Arafat

ADAM AND EVE

Muslims believe that the idea of Hajj goes right back to the Adam and Eve, the first man and woman.

According to tradition, Adam and Eve were tempted by the devil to disobey God. God sent them out of their lovely paradise (the Garden of Eden). They lost each other and wandered the earth, very unhappy.

God watched over them, waiting for them to realize their error and come back to Him, asking for forgiveness. At last, they prayed for forgiveness and God received them back.

The reunion took place on a small mountain called Jabal ar-Rahman, or the Mount of Mercy, in the plain of Arafat. They built a simple shrine nearby in gratitude to God.

Now Muslims celebrate this event as part of Hajj. They hope, like Adam and Eve, to be forgiven all their past sins and gain the promise of paradise.

IBRAHIM

The second tradition concerns the moment when God tested Ibrahim's loyalty.

Ibrahim was a wealthy man who owned many sheep and goats. He was humble and devoted to God. He lived with his first wife, Sarah, who was childless, and a second wife, **Hajar** who had given him a son, **Isma'il**.

In a dream, Ibrahim heard God asking him to sacrifice his most beloved only son, Isma'il. When he awoke he told his son the dream.

THE TEST

Isma'il was terrified, but told his father that he must obey God '…and do not worry about me'. Although they did not understand *why* God wanted them to do this, they accepted that it was God's will and must be obeyed.

The family set out for **Mina**, the place of sacrifices. On the way, the devil appeared in human form to tempt them to doubt the dream. Each argument seemed so reasonable that it made the sacrifice seem even harder.

- Surely it was the devil asking Ibrahim to do such a wicked act? God would never ask it.

- How could Hajar let Ibrahim do this to their only boy? Didn't Ibrahim love his wife and wasn't he willing to do anything she asked?

- Didn't Isma'il realize his father was mad? Isma'il should run away and not let himself get killed like a fool!

All three resisted the temptations. According to tradition, Ibrahim picked up stones and threw them at the stranger to drive him away.

THE SACRIFICE

When they reached the appointed place, Isma'il said, 'Put me face downwards.' He did not want his father to hesitate when he saw his face. Ibrahim lay him on the altar and did not even have to tie him down. Both were consenting to the sacrifice.

At the last moment, God stopped Ibrahim. As a reward for his obedience his other wife, Sarah, gave birth to a son, Isaac. Isma'il was the founder of the Arab tribes, and Isaac the founder of the Jews (see surah 37:100–113).

HAJAR'S THIRST

Sarah grew jealous on behalf of her son. God told Ibrahim he should take Hajar and Isma'il to the ancient shrine in the plain of Arafat and leave them there in God's care.

The desert was barren and waterless. Hajar and Isma'il were dying of thirst – it seemed that God had abandoned them. Hajar ran frantically between the two hills of **Safa** and **Marwah** in search of water, but found none.

At the last moment, the angel Jibril appeared and showed her a spring at the feet of Isma'il. This spring is now known as the **Zamzam well**.

MAKKAH

Later the family got back together and Ibrahim and Isma'il built a small square-walled shrine from rough stone. To lay the top layers, Ibrahim stood on a large rock, the **Maqam Ibrahim**. This building became known as the Ka'bah, or Cube, a very holy place.

A village of tents soon appeared around the well, and the town of Makkah was set up there.

For around 4000 years the Ka'bah has been rebuilt on the same foundation, and has been a centre for pilgrimage.

TALKING POINTS

- Do you think true believers should always trust God and obey Him without question? What does this kind of trust involve?

- How should believers deal with temptations and tests of the devil?

FOR YOUR FOLDERS

1 What do you think these stories teach Muslims about their faith?

   a Adam and Eve.
   b The testing of Ibrahim and his family.
   c The sacrifice of Isma'il.
   d The testing of Hajar in the desert.

2 How does the Ka'bah remind Muslims of the idea of complete submission (obedience) to God?

Hajj pilgrims in the Safa–Marwah walkway

IHRAM

When pilgrims draw near to Makkah, they must enter the state of **ihram**. This means they must concentrate totally on worship and prayer. Pilgrims must also be humble and turn away from ideas of vanity. Male pilgrims wear two sheets of plain white cloth – one wrapped round the waist, the other over the left shoulder. Women wear a plain white garment that covers them, leaving only their hands and faces bare. All pilgrims dress alike to symbolize that they are equal before God.

Ihram also reminds Muslims that in death all symbols of rank and wealth are left behind.

Other rules for pilgrims

- Do not do anything dishonest or arrogant.

- Do not think about the opposite sex; Muslims may not get engaged to marry on Hajj; sex, even between married couples, is set aside for the time.

- Men must not wear jewellery or rings.

- No one may use perfume or scented soap.

- Men must not cover their heads. This is an act of humility. (They can use an umbrella against the sun's heat.)

- Women may not cover their faces. This is to show confidence that all impure thoughts have been put aside.

- No one must cut hair or finger nails, so as not to interfere with nature.

- To show love for nature, no plants may be pulled up nor trees cut down.

- To express simplicity, everyone must go barefoot or in sandals.

- To show unity with God's creatures, there must be no blood shed in killing animals (except pests such as fleas, snakes and scorpions). No hunting is allowed.

- Muslims must not show aggression.

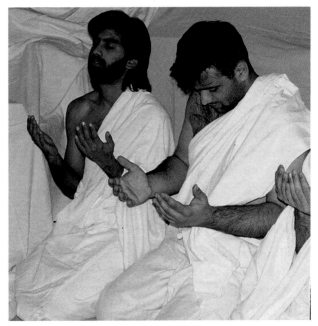

Pilgrims in a state of ihram

Muslims must try their hardest to keep their minds at peace and not lose their tempers, quarrel or get upset by difficulties.

As pilgrims approach Makkah, they recite the prayer, called the talbiyah, over and over again:

> Here I am, O God, here I am!
> I am here, O Thou without equal,
> here I am!
>
> Thine is the kingdom,
> the praise and the glory,
>
> Thou without equal, God Alone!

Muslims believe that by making the pilgrimage they are responding to God's call and this prayer expresses their feelings. Some shout the prayer joyfully, while others are overcome with emotion and may weep.

Pilgrims feel that each one of them is important to God and that God has seen each one of them arrive. It is a humbling experience.

Here is another pilgrim prayer.

O God,
this sanctuary is Your sacred place,
and this city is Your city,
and this slave is Your slave.

I have come to You from a distant land,
carrying all my sins and misdeeds
as an afflicted person seeking Your help
and dreading Your punishment.

I beg You to accept me,
and grant me Your complete forgiveness,
and give me permission to enter
Your vast garden of delight.

THE CIRCLING

On arrival in Makkah the pilgrims hurry to the Ka'bah and go round it seven times quickly, running if possible. This is called **tawaf** and expresses love for God.

As they arrive they call out 'At Your command, our Lord, at Your command!'

If possible, pilgrims try to kiss or touch the Black Stone in its recess in the wall of the Ka'bah. If they cannot reach it because of the crowds, they each raise their hand towards it in salute every time they go past it. They say a prayer each time they pass.

Next, pilgrims walk seven times between Safa and Marwah in memory of Hajar's search for water.

During the pilgrimage, women uncover their faces, trusting in the purity of men's thoughts

THINKING POINTS

- Why do you think that pilgrims on Hajj seem to be so happy and excited?

- Why do you think the cloths worn for ihram later become treasured possessions?

FOR YOUR FOLDERS

1 Imagine you are a Muslim returning from Hajj. Write a letter to a friend describing some of the things you must or must not do while in a state of ihram. Explain what this experience has meant to you.

2 Write out one of the two prayers in this unit. You could do this as a decorated scroll or poster.

3 Explain what ihram and tawaf mean.

4 What is the significance of Muslim women not covering their faces during Hajj?

1 – The Great Mosque
2 – The Ka'bah
3 – Mina
4 – Muzdalifah
5 – Plain of Arafat
6 – The Mount of Mercy

The route of Hajj

BAITULLAH

The Ka'bah is also known as **Baitullah**, the House of Allah. This plain, cube-shaped building made of blocks is not very pretty. However, Muslims claim that it is on the site of the oldest shrine to God on earth, built originally by Adam. It was rebuilt by Ibrahim and Isma'il.

When the Prophet captured Makkah he broke up the idols of 360 other 'gods' that were in the Ka'bah.

Now the inside of the Ka'bah is a plain room, decorated with texts from the Qur'an. Sometimes special visitors are allowed inside the Ka'bah, to stand at its centre and pray in all four directions.

AL-KISWAH

The Ka'bah is covered by a black cloth called the **kiswah**. This is embroidered in gold and silver thread with texts from the Qur'an. At the end of Hajj it is cut up and pilgrims can take pieces as a memento of the experience of a lifetime. A new kiswah is prepared every year.

THE BLACK STONE

This is an oval rock about 18cm in diameter, set in the south-east corner of the Ka'bah. It is cased in a silver frame and marks the start of the walk circling the shrine. Pilgrims try to touch or kiss it. Pre-Islamic traditions say that:

- the stone was dug out of the earth by Isma'il from a place shown to him by the angel Jibril
- Jibril brought it from paradise and gave it to Adam
- it was given to the descendants of Nuh (Noah) after the flood.

The stone is certainly ancient, and was mentioned by the writer Maximus of Tyre in 2 CE. It is probably a meteorite.

MARWAH AND SAFA

These are the two small hills between which Hajar ran when she desperately tried to find water for her son, Isma'il. Now the hills are enclosed under domes and joined by a walkway.

ZAMZAM

The angel Jibril showed Hajar a spring of water near the place where she had laid Isma'il. The tradition is that the water came from the place where his heels dug into the sand as he tossed about in a fever. Hajar called the well Zamzam. For Muslims, it symbolizes the truth that when all seems lost, God still cares for His people.

The well of Zamzam is in the courtyard of the Great Mosque in Makkah. Pilgrims collect water from it to drink and to take home. Many dip their white garments in it, then keep them to be used for their burial shrouds.

ARAFAT

Mount Arafat is the Mount of Mercy where God reunited Adam and Eve. Here about two million people camp (see unit 32) and stand before God.

MUZDALIFAH

Pilgrims camp at **Muzdalifah** on their journey between Arafat and Makkah. They pick up pebbles to hurl at the pillars of Mina.

MINA

The pillars here represent the place where Ibrahim and his family faced temptations and stoned the devil. The Saudi Arabian Ministry of Pilgrimage has built a huge walkway to Mina.

THINGS TO DO

Write a sentence or two about what is significant, or what is done, at the following places.

Ka'bah shrine	Black Stone
Safa and Marwah	Zamzam
Mount Arafat	Muzdalifah
Mina	

Pilgrims throw stones at the pillar that represents Iblis (the devil)

Entering the Ka'bah

The road to Mina

On the morning of 9 Dhul-Hijjah, pilgrims leave Mina and set off for Mount Arafat – a day's journey on foot. Many pilgrims today miss out Mina and go straight to Arafat because of the huge numbers involved.

THE STAND

At the Mount of Mercy in the plain of Arafat the pilgrims stand before God to make their **wuquf**. They stand from noon to sunset, meditating and praying, thinking only of God. Everyone must do this, or the Hajj is not valid.

Muslims find this a great mystical experience. They believe their sins have been washed away and they feel they can start anew, totally cleansed.

A rocky path leads to the top of Arafat, where pilgrims may listen to a sermon. Then they spend the night in the open, praying and expressing their thanks to God. After this, Muslims may go home, feeling they have been released from their sins.

Returning Muslims spend the night of 10 Dhul-Hijjah at Muzdalifah. Before dawn, they again stand before God. Just before dawn breaks, the pilgrims depart for Mina.

COMMENT

To have stood before God at Arafat is like having a baby. You have either had the experience or you have not. No one can truly explain how it feels – but those who know it, know. Perhaps those whose hearts God has seized can understand.

(a woman pilgrim's comment)

TALKING POINT

A pilgrim on Hajj is like a drop of water in an ocean. In such a mass of people, why is Hajj such an intensely personal experience?

Pilgrims stand before God at Mount Arafat

THE UNFURLING

The rest of the pilgrimage is called the unfurling.

At Mina the pilgrims throw stones at the pillars to show their rejection of the devil.

Next, on 10 Dhul-Hijjah the Feast of Sacrifice (**Id-ul-Adha** – see page 80) begins. Every pilgrim must sacrifice an animal. The feast lasts two or three days. Nowadays, with about two million pilgrims, it is impossible to eat all the meat, even if it is shared among the poor. The Saudi authorities arrange for carcases to be frozen so they can be distributed later.

After the sacrifice, men have their heads shaved and women cut off about 2.5cm of their hair. Ihram is now over.

The pilgrims then return to Makkah for one last circling of the Ka'bah. Now it is more like a holiday!

Finally, they visit Zamzam to dip their white cloths in its water. Many drink deeply from it, in the belief that it cures diseases. They take some home for their families, together with their souvenir pieces of the Black Cloth. They can now take the name Hajji or Hajjah.

Shaving heads when Hajj is complete

MUSLIM TOURISM

After the Hajj most pilgrims go to visit the Prophet's tomb at Madinah. They may visit the mosque that was the Prophet's home and the room of his youngest wife Aishah, which is behind it. They may see the graves of the Prophet's companions, Abu Bakr and Umar. There is also a tradition that there is a place reserved there for Isa after his second coming.

There are other places of interest: Mount Nur, where the Prophet first saw the angel; Mount Thawr where he sheltered from the Quraish; the battle-sites and the Masjid at-Taqwa where the Prophet built a mosque when he entered Madinah.

They may visit the simple tombs of **Uthman**, Aishah and Hasan in the cemetery of al-Baqee.

THINGS TO DO

Imagine you have been all night in the vast crowd at wuquf. Dawn is breaking. Write a paragraph describing what you might feel.

FOR YOUR FOLDERS

Explain how, for a Muslim, Hajj:

a brings 'release' and inner peace

b builds up courage and trust in God

c draws all Muslims together

d unites Muslims not only with each other but with their beloved prophets of the past.

FESTIVALS

The Muslim word for a festival is 'id' or 'eid'.

During festivals Muslims praise God and thank Him for His goodness. They remember loved ones who are far from home, or those who have died. It is a time to forgive enemies and to renew contacts with people they have not seen for a long time.

People must be kind to the poor, the lonely and the stranger. Orphans must feel loved and cared for. Lazy people must make an effort to make up for things they have not done, and hostile people must make peace.

DATES

Muslim festivals are not always on the same date each year. This is because in the Islamic calendar months are calculated according to the moon (lunar months), and the Islamic year is about eleven days shorter than the solar (sun-based) year. So Muslim festivals come eleven days earlier each year.

The two most important festivals are Id-ul-Adha (see unit 39), the feast of sacrifice during Hajj, and Id-ul-Fitr (see unit 38), the feast that marks the end of Ramadan's month-long fast. There are six other special days for Muslims.

MAWLID AN-NABI

Mawlid an-Nabi is the birthday of the Prophet, probably originally 20 August 570 CE. There are joyful processions and stories told of Muhammad's life and work.

LAYLAT-UL-QADR

Laylat-ul-Qadr celebrates the Night of Power when the Prophet received his first revelation of the Qur'an (see unit 3). It is held during the last ten days of the Ramadan fast. Usually there is a special event on 27 Ramadan, when Muslims may stay up all night, praying and reciting the Qur'an.

LAYLAT-UL-MI'RAJ

Laylat-ul-Mi'raj recalls the night when the Prophet made the night journey to Jerusalem and into the presence of God (see unit 6). Muslims remember that it was during this special moment that the five daily prayers were fixed.

LAYLAT-UL-BARA'AT

Laylat-ul-Bara'at is the night of the full moon before the start of Ramadan, and marks the time when the Prophet used to begin his preparations for Ramadan by praying all night. Many Muslims stay awake all night and read the Qur'an as part of their celebration.

Regent's Park mosque, in London, has no room for these worshipper, so they must say Id prayers outside

MUHARRAM

Muharram is the first month of the Muslim calendar. New Year's Day is celebrated when the new moon appears. This celebrates the Hijrah, the journey of the Prophet to Madinah. Muslims date their years from this event, so the year after the Hijrah is 1 AH. For Muslims it is an opportunity to move on from their past – to leave their old failings behind them and make a fresh start with new year resolutions.

10 MUHARRAM OR ASHURA

This was already a traditional day of fasting before the time of the Prophet. It has links with the Jewish Day of Atonement. In Muslim tradition it also recalls the day when Nuh (Noah) left the Ark after the flood, and the day on which God saved Musa (Moses) from Pharaoh. Some Muslims fast in the day, then enjoy a special meal at night.

For **Shi'ite** Muslims this marks the day when the Prophet's grandson **Husayn** was killed.

Ashura in New York, USA – Shi'ites in mourning

Shi'ites express great grief publicly, and some men beat themselves with chains and cut themselves with swords to share the sufferings of Husayn.

THINGS TO DO

To find the year in the Muslim calendar:
subtract 622 from the year in the calendar we use and multiply it by $\frac{33}{32}$, e.g.

$$\text{CE } 1902 = (1902 - 622) \times \tfrac{33}{32}$$
$$= 1280 \times \tfrac{33}{32}$$
$$= 1320 \text{ AH}$$

What is the Muslim year for 2001 CE?

FOR YOUR FOLDERS

1 Write a list of the *six* special days in Islam and say briefly what each one stands for.

2 'The special days remember the Prophet, they don't remember God.' Do you agree? Give reasons for your answer, showing that you have thought carefully about it.

TALKING POINT

The Prophet was a very modest and humble man. How do you think he would have liked people to honour his memory?

THE PREPARATION

Id-ul-Fitr comes at the end of Ramadan, the month of fasting. Everyone gets very excited as they wait to catch a glimpse of the new moon, when the festivities can begin. But families must prepare well in advance. They must:

- buy food and prepare it well beforehand (sometimes Muslim shops stay open very late for the few days before)
- buy decorations and hang them up
- buy or make Id cards, and send them to relatives and friends
- prepare gifts and sweets for the children
- paint and decorate houses
- collect money for the poor.

This is the last day for sending **Zakat-ul-Fitr**, a special form of Zakah (see unit 30) during Ramadan.

All dressed up for Id

THE ANNOUNCEMENT

Originally Id-ul-Fitr was announced by the call to prayer from the mosque. Now the time is announced on radio and television. In the West the news is sent to mosques by radio, fax and telephone.

As soon as the signal comes, everyone dashes out to greet each other, with handshakes and hugs and cries of 'Id Mubarak!' or 'Happy Id'. It is a time for celebration for completing a successful fast.

In memory of Muhammad, Muslims break the fast with a simple snack of dates or a drink. One popular drink, made from apricots, is called 'moon of religion'.

The family then prays together and returns to the table to enjoy a celebration meal.

ID DAY

There is a three-day public holiday in Muslim countries. In non-Muslim countries, some understanding employers allow a day off.

THE ROUTINE

Celebrations include the following.

- Taking a bath or shower.
- Putting on new or best clothes.
- Gathering in the largest mosque, or a park or playing field – some congregations have thousands of people.
- Encouraging women and children to come – though many mothers are too busy at home getting things ready.
- Everyone praying together – the sermon is usually about the importance of giving.
- More greetings and hugs, then visits to houses of friends and family. Children get presents and pocket money. There is a special midday dinner – the first meal eaten in daylight for over a month! There may be many 'sittings' as people come

and go. Everyone helps with supplies and cooking.

- Visits to the cemetery to remember loved ones who have died.
- Visits that go on well into the night – no one wants to leave anyone out, and the celebrations go on late into the night.

QUICK QUIZ

1 What is the Muslim word for festival?

2 Which month ends with Id-ul-Fitr?

3 What must be seen before Id can begin?

4 What money must be paid now?

5 How does the Id congregation differ from the usual ones?

THINGS TO DO

1 Design and draw your own Id card.

2 Make a list of the things you would have to do to celebrate Id in your own house.

FOR YOUR FOLDERS

1 In what ways does Id-ul-Fitr bring Muslims close together as

   a individual families

   b a whole community?

2 Why do you think children specially enjoy Id-ul-Fitr?

3 What do you think is the importance of festivals to a religion? What might happen if festivals ceased to be regularly celebrated?

Greeting each other with a hug and 'Id Mubarak' – the blessings of Id

Id card

Id-ul-Adha is the most important festival in the Islamic year and is held in the Hajj month. It celebrates the way that Ibrahim's faith was strong enough to let him resist the devil and remain obedient to God. For Muslims taking part in the festival it stands for their own obedience, and it renews their faithfulness to God.

This is a feast for all Muslims, not just those on Hajj. Families and the whole community of Muslims can join in. It is a serious event, and focuses on sacrifice. The sacrificing of an animal represents personal self-sacrifice.

In Muslim countries there is a national holiday for four days when schools, shops and offices are closed. Streets are deserted as families visit each other at home.

The feast represents the readiness of Muslims to sacrifice all their own wants and needs, even life itself, to the service of God.

> Neither the flesh of the animals of your sacrifice nor their blood reach Allah – it is your righteousness that reaches Him.

(surah 22:37)

PREPARATIONS

These begin well in advance. Families buy gifts and new clothes. They must buy and prepare food for the big day. A suitable animal must be chosen for the sacrifice. It might be a sheep, goat, cow or camel. The animals must be bought two or three weeks before the feast day.

THE SACRIFICE

When possible the animals are looked after at home. Muslims – especially children – can become fond of the animals.

It is one thing if a butcher kills an animal. It is entirely different if you have to do it yourself. This makes it possible for Muslims to understand how hard it was for Ibrahim to pass his test when he thought he had to kill his own son.

It is a duty for Muslims to know how to kill an animal quickly and kindly, and to take responsibility for it.

If possible, the animal must be calm and not frightened. Its throat is cut with a very sharp knife across the jugular vein and it loses consciousness very quickly. Prayers are said while this is being done.

Sacrificing a sheep at the slaughterhouse

All dressed up for Id

In the West, a special licence is needed to kill an animal. Nowadays most families have their feast animals killed at an abattoir (slaughterhouse) by a licence holder. In Britain this is the law.

Sometimes Muslims who have recently moved to this country, and do not know this law, might sacrifice goats in their home.

The meat is divided up for the poor, for friends and relatives and for the family to use. In some countries, Id-ul-Adha is the only time in the year when poor people get meat to eat.

Instead of meat, money can be donated to the poor.

FOR YOUR FOLDERS

1 Try to explain how the feast of Id-ul-Adha is part of the Hajj for all Muslims, whether they are on Hajj or at home.

2 What does Id-ul-Adha celebrate?

3 How does a Muslim relate the sacrifice of an animal to the sacrifice he or she might have to make for their religion?

4 How could a Muslim show readiness to love and serve God in normal daily life?

5 Are there any things or people you would be prepared to sacrifice your life for?

FOR DISCUSSION

● 'Having to sacrifice an animal teaches compassion and responsibility.'

● 'You can't learn about duty and obedience without facing the hardship of performing them.'

Shari'ah means 'path'. Muslims believe that God has set out a path for them to follow. It is a code of behaviour.

> This is my straight path, so follow it, and do not follow [other] paths which will separate you from this path.

> (surah 6:153)

TAQWA

From the moment a Muslim becomes aware of God the most important questions are 'What shall I do now? How shall I live?' This awareness of God is called taqwa (see unit 4).

Being in a state of taqwa changes things for Muslims. It means giving up their selfish ways and even changing the way they think. The aim of Shari'ah is to find the best way of living for the benefit of everyone.

JUSTICE

Muslims believe that the laws in society should be fair and just, and everyone should obey them. In Muslim countries, the laws must be based on the rules set out by the Prophet (see unit 8).

Muslims believe that people must start by living right lives themselves. True justice can never come about until the whole of society follows the will of God. For this to happen, those trying to live holy lives must continue to live within the community. They must not shut themselves off from the world. They must find the right path, the Shari'ah, and help others to follow it.

Shari'ah is the law that sets out what is right (**halal**) and what is wrong (**haram**) in any particular case. It covers all aspects of life.

THE PRINCIPLES BEHIND SHARI'AH

- God exists.
- There is life after death, and all people will be judged.

Everyone will be judged

- God is aware of all you do and think.
- The hardships of the world should be put right and not just ignored.

UMMAH

Muslims believe that everyone belongs to God and all people are equal. Race, nationality, status or wealth should not matter. There should be family feeling among all people – comforting one another when in trouble, rejoicing with each other when happy.

This feeling of family closeness is called **ummah**.

FOLLOWING SHARI'AH

Following Shari'ah means living a morally responsible life. All humans should:

> hold tight to the rope which God [stretches out for you] and do not be divided amongst yourselves. …He united your hearts together in love, so that by His grace you became brothers.

> (surah 3:103)

If humans can live as though everyone is one big family, they have already started living according to Shari'ah.

Muslims believe we are all one family

What will teach you what the steep highway is? It is to ransom the captive, to feed the orphan or the poor who lie in the dust.

(surah 90:12–16)

If any single part of the body aches, the whole body feels the effects and rushes to its relief.

Everyone of you is a shepherd, and will be questioned about the well-being of his flock.

(Hadiths)

Muslims have no time for *hypocrites* – people who make a show of religion, but are selfish, lazy or mean.

Leading a moral life helps to bring about self-confidence and strength. The ideals are: love of God; humility; modesty; naturalness and unselfishness. This will help to promote the happiness and welfare of society.

THE FIVE SCHOOLS

In the ninth and tenth centuries CE, Muslim rulers asked the leading teachers to write down the Islamic Law in detail. There were five main schools of law, named after their leading imams: Jafar al-Sadiq, Malik, Abu Hanifa, Shafi'i and Ahmad ibn Hanbal. Most Muslims today follow one of these schools.

CLOSED OR OPEN?

Muslims who think that these schools of law covered everything necessary, say that 'the gate of knowledge is *closed*'. Others who feel that modern society with its particular problems needs a new approach say that 'the gate should be left *open*'. This argument causes division between 'modernist' and 'fundamentalist' Muslims (see unit 69).

THINKING POINTS

- Why do Muslims think religious people should live in ordinary society?

- Why do you think Muslims believe God requires modesty and unselfishness?

- Is being 'equal in the sight of God' the same as 'being equal'?

FOR YOUR FOLDERS

1 What is taqwa? How does taqwa affect a Muslim's life?

2 Why do you think Muslims believe that a truly just society must be based on the Will of God?

3 Explain why many Muslims feel it is important to 'keep the gate open'.

THINGS TO DO

Try to interview a Muslim to find out what it is like living according to Shari'ah in your community.

The Qur'an gives Muslims the Shari'ah, which they must accept without question. They have further guidance by following the example of Muhammad, called Sunnah.

PROBLEMS

How can a law set down over a thousand years ago in Arabia answer questions raised by today's science and technology? How can a person know what is right for them in this present age? Should they bother to look any further than the law of the land? Why should God (if there is one) bother with such matters?

This is not the way Muslims think. They cannot accept the idea of a society without God. God *does* care and He can help humans in the task of living their lives.

FREEDOM

When Muslims submit to God, they accept *all* the revealed laws. They cannot say that one law is more important than another.

In submitting to God, a person is free from all other things. A person is no longer a servant of another person, a set of ideas, or of objects (possessions) or of institutions. A person who submits to God becomes God's Khalifa, or steward, on earth (see unit 15).

QIYAS

Qiyas is a way of working out Muslim principles by *analogy*. Any Muslim has the right to use their own judgement to decide whether an action is right according to the spirit of the Qur'an and Hadiths, when there is no set guidance.

The decisions made by the teachers of the past are called **ijma**. The only ijma that Muslims must obey are those reached by the Prophet's original Companions. Later ijma based on other opinions can be accepted as guidelines, but they are not binding. The forming of an individual's opinion is called **ijtihad**.

Shi'ite imams (see unit 72) known as **mujtahids** – living religious scholars – or chief imams, **ayatollahs** or 'shadows of God' claim the right to exercise ijtihad. They say only scholars can do this. Sufis feel that any religious person has this right (see unit 73).

PRINCIPLES

People making decisions must take account of:

- the opinions of respected people
- previous decisions
- justice and concern for the good of the people
- the acceptance of the masses.

LIMITS

The principles behind Shari'ah are there to deter various pressure groups from imposing too great a burden on people. These burdens may go beyond the spirit of Islam. There must be a range of opportunities to solve problems. Islam does not encourage fanaticism. No one could add a sixth prayer during the day or charge extra zakah. Any Muslim would have the right to challenge this and demand to see the basis for it in the Qur'an or Hadiths.

The aim of Shari'ah is to provide guidance about God's will in any new or changed situation.

RULES OF BEHAVIOUR

There are five kinds of behaviour:

- things that *must* be done, e.g. prayer, fasting in Ramadan
- recommended actions, e.g. unselfish hospitality, extra prayers, forgiveness
- actions to be decided by conscience where there is no clear guidance

- actions disapproved of, e.g. divorce, smoking
- forbidden things (haram), e.g. worshipping false Gods, adultery.

Modern Muslims must use their conscience. What is not forbidden is allowed, under the guidance of your conscience. If an action is harmful to yourself or others, it cannot be recommended by a Muslim.

MODERNISM AND FUNDAMENTALISM

If Muslims use qiyas and ijtihad properly, it is possible to have fresh ideas on past decisions and keep up with the changing world. **Modernist Muslims** think this is vital.

Fresh thinking on past decisions

They think that it is wrong to neglect today's great scholars and thinkers.

Fundamentalist Muslims, however, want only the original teachings and see all modern views as 'innovations'.

THINKING POINTS

- How would Muslims respond to unjust laws being introduced? What principles would they take into account?
- Why do you think Muslims think 'small laws' are as important as 'more serious' laws?

QUICK QUIZ

1 What is meant by the Sunnah?

2 What is ijtihad?

3 Give an example of a recommended action.

4 Give an example of something that needs to be decided by conscience.

FOR YOUR FOLDERS

1 Explain what the five kinds of behaviour are. Which do you think is the largest area? How are the rules worked out for that area?

2 How can submission to God be seen as freedom?

3 Why are qiyas important to a modernist Muslim? Why might they be resisted by a fundamentalist?

It is very important for Muslims to show active concern and hospitality to others, whether they are members of their own family or strangers. They must be kind, respectful, patient, understanding, slow to anger, and modest. Allah instructs them to be kind to those who seek help, eager to visit friends, to visit the sick or those in prison and to comfort the bereaved.

EATING TOGETHER

Muslims are always glad to invite visitors for meals, as eating together strengthens social ties. The many feasts and parties to celebrate festivals and family events are opportunities to give the less well-off a treat. Muslims do not approve of feasts where only wealthy people are invited.

CLEANLINESS

Personal purity (**taharah**) is important to Muslims. As well as wudu (see unit 25), they bathe frequently, paying particular attention to body odours – mouth, feet, underarms and private parts.

When they are still very young, children learn how to use a toothbrush, and that they should keep their clothes clean. They must avoid dogs and street dirt. Muslims are very particular about personal hygiene after going to the toilet or during the monthly period. They usually wash with water – Muslim toilets always have a water supply. Muslims visiting Britain for the first time are often upset when they find toilets that have no water for washing.

Muslims bathe the whole body after sexual intercourse (and, out of consideration for their partner, before as well). They also bathe after childbirth and menstruation. They are also encouraged to bathe after contact with a dead body.

The Prophet recommended that Muslims should cut nails short and keep them very clean, and that they should shave off all the hair from under their arms and their private parts.

As Muslims wash their feet five times a day, they never worry about taking their socks off in public! At home, carpets are kept spotless and ready to use for prayer. So Muslims usually take off their shoes when entering a carpeted room.

TABLE MANNERS

Silver or gold tableware is considered too flashy. Cooking pans, plates and glasses are always spotless and shining. Meals are usually simple and healthy, often based on stews or curries with rice, with enough for an unexpected guest. Muslims may eat with their hands and not use cutlery – especially if there are lots of guests. They invite guests as often as possible.

Before eating, Muslims bless the food saying, 'In the name of Allah, the Compassionate, the Merciful.'

Children must not start eating before their parents, and hosts should not start before guests. No one speaks with their mouth full, or reads while eating. People should take food from the nearest side offered. It is not polite to complain or find fault. Muslims try to finish the meal and leave the table together.

Sometimes the hostess does not eat with the others but serves them and eats afterwards.

A healthy stew…

Greeting one another at the mosque

GREETINGS

Muslims greet each other with 'Peace be with you'. The reply is 'And on you be peace'.

Men may hug and kiss each other but women are not expected to touch men who are not related to them. Muslim men do not usually shake hands with women, and would never embrace or try to kiss them.

AT WORK

Muslim women discourage men from being too familiar or making sexual remarks at work. They take it as their right not to be sexually harassed.

FOR DISCUSSION

- Should a Muslim mother with guests object to being treated 'like a servant'?
- Are people who sit on the floor and eat with their hands dirty?

VISITORS

Muslims believe they should knock and wait for a reply when visiting others unannounced. If they knock three times without answer, they should leave without being offended that no one has answered.

The Prophet disapproved of people invading the privacy of others. He once said that people who spied on the homes of others should have their eyes poked out!

MANNERS

Muslims say:

- 'If Allah wishes' when hoping to do something
- 'Glory to God' to praise someone
- 'As Allah wills' in appreciation of something
- 'May Allah give you the best reward' when thanking someone
- 'Praise be to Allah' when they wish to give thanks
- 'O Allah forgive me' to show sorrow for a bad action.

FOR YOUR FOLDERS

1 How does the idea of taharah affect Muslim life?

2 Some people might think Muslims are afraid of dogs, or are dirty to eat with their hands. How would a Muslim reply?

3 Imagine you were going to practise taharah for a day. Make a diary of events, from when you get up in the morning until you go to bed.

MODESTY IN DRESS

> Say to believing men that they should lower their gaze and guard their modesty …and that believing women should lower their gaze and guard their modesty;…that they should draw their veils over their bosoms and not display their beauty except to their close male relatives.

> (surah 24:30–1. The surah gives a precise list of relatives)

Muslim women outside the home should try not to draw attention to themselves. If a man tries to catch their eye, they should not stare at him but look away. The Qur'an teaches that modesty in dress will ensure that a woman is not molested or annoyed by men.

The Shari'ah tries to keep high standards in societies that are becoming more immoral. It teaches that women should wear clothes that are not too revealing or too colourful. This does not mean a Muslim woman must always wear a black, tent-like garment (**chador** – see opposite). In fact, millions simply dress in a modest way.

Muslim women should not show themselves off. They should not wear clothes that are low-cut, short, see-through or tight. They believe that this would stir up male passion – which is unfair to both sexes.

Passion that runs out of control causes trouble and hurts people. So a woman who deliberately leads a man to temptation has a bad reputation. Muslims consider sex within marriage to be healthy and wholesome. They believe too much sexual freedom harms individuals, upsets parents, and results in unwanted children and broken marriages. So it is important to be careful in behaviour and dress.

Muslim women, like most others, want to be appreciated for their minds and characters, not just for their bodies. Modest dress helps to bring this about as it discourages lust in men.

Muslim women usually cover their heads, necks and throats with a scarf or veil. They wear clothes that cover their arms and legs. This is called wearing **hijab**. Hijab does not prevent women going out on business or taking an active part in society. Female dress in the West was modest, too, until the twentieth century.

Ideally, a woman should not behave and dress because of pressure from relatives or society, but because she herself wishes to please God. Indeed, many Muslim women continue to wear hijab even though their husbands or governments oppose it.

In practice, many Muslim women prefer the traditional long dress and head-veil because:

- it is easy and practical
- it covers up the results of increasing age and weight gain, pregnancy etc.
- it is graceful and feminine without being sexy.

PURDAH

In many countries women and men live completely separate lives. Women cover themselves completely, including their faces. This is not part of Islam, but is purely local custom. Indeed many people of other religions follow these rules. This social separation and dressing so that the body and face are not visible is called **purdah**.

When women do not want to talk to strangers, wearing a chador gives them privacy. They can get on with their business without being disturbed or made the object of unwanted attention.

Iranian woman wearing chador

Wearing hijab

MALE CLOTHING

The Qur'an requires men to be modest, clean and smart. When praying, they must always be covered at least from waist to knees.

They may not wear silk, or gold jewellery. They can wear any style of clothing, but basically should not be overdressed or flashy. They should not show bare legs, chests or arms. They do not have to wear turbans, head-cloths or white lace caps.

> Modesty and faith are joined closely together; if either of them is lost, the other goes also.
>
> (Hadith)

FOR DISCUSSION

Should a female Western tourist walk through Muslim streets wearing shorts and a sun-top? What reaction might she expect if she does so? What about male tourists wearing shorts and open shirts?

FOR YOUR FOLDERS

1 People often think that veiled women are treated as inferior to men. What are the real aims of Muslim clothing?

2 Should Muslims who come to live in the West accept Western customs and give up their own?

3 What do Muslim women think are the advantages of hijab? Why might dressing like this not appeal to all women?

Brechin High School

89

HARAM AND HALAL

For Muslims even eating is dedicated to God. His will must be obeyed, so the basic need to eat is a discipline. The Qur'an says that certain foods are 'haram' or forbidden. Any food that is not haram is allowed. Food that is allowed is called 'halal'. The unlawful foods include:

- any product made from a pig (pork, bacon, etc.)
- meat that has blood in it
- meat from an animal that 'died of itself' due to disease or old age
- any flesh-eating animal
- any animal that has been strangled, beaten to death, killed by a fall, killed by another animal, or partly eaten by another animal
- any animal sacrificed to idols (see surah 5:3–4).

Muslims think that meat with congealed blood in it is disgusting. If an animal dies by one of the means above, its blood will have congealed in it. Similar laws to these apply to Jews and to the early Christians (see Acts 15:29).

HALAL KILLING

Animals that may be eaten must be killed according to the halal (permitted) method. That is, the jugular vein in the neck must be cut with a sharp knife while the butcher calls on the name of God.

Sometimes non-Muslims may think this method of killing is cruel, even though they may not know how their own meat is killed. Muslims consider this method as being the kindest, and refuse to eat meat killed any other way.

Muslims regard electrocution and shooting as cruel methods of killing animals. They also disapprove of factory farming and experiments on animals. Muslim butchers call on the name of God to show that they are not taking life carelessly but for food, with the permission of God to whom all life belongs.

Most people do not like the idea of killing animals at all and would not like to do it themselves. They say that stunning the animal first with an electric shock is better. Muslims consider that passing a high voltage electric current through an animal's brain so that it will not feel the knife simply doesn't make sense.

Muslim attitudes to alcohol and tobacco are discussed in unit 68.

THINKING POINT

What is the intention behind halal killing? Why might a Muslim not be shocked by the thought of killing a sheep in his or her garden? Why might such an action offend people in the West?

Halal butcher's shop

PERMITTED FOODS

Muslims are allowed to eat fish, poultry, sheep, goats and camels, and game caught by hunting animals that are trained for this purpose. The name of God is pronounced when the hawk or dog releases the animal. Chicken is a favourite meat.

All fruit, grains and vegetables are allowed. If nothing else is available, Muslims are permitted to eat anything edible.

> O ye who believe! Eat of the good things that We have provided for you, and be grateful to God if it is Him you worship. He has only forbidden you meat of an animal that dies of itself, and blood, and the flesh of pigs,…But if one is forced because there is no other choice, then one can eat other food without being guilty.
>
> (surah 2:172–3, see also surahs 5:4 and 6:145)

The Qur'an suggests that meat butchered by Jews or Christians may also be allowed.

> This day are all things good and pure made lawful to you. The food of the People of the Book is lawful to you, and yours is lawful to them.
>
> (surah 5:6)

SOCIAL CONSEQUENCES IN NON-MUSLIM SOCIETY

The food laws may affect Muslims' ability to mix socially with their non-Muslim neighbours. Nearly all meat in the West is killed by electrocution or by firing a bolt into the animal's brain. It is therefore forbidden to Muslims. They must not buy meat from a market unless they know it is halal. If they cannot get halal meat, they are obliged to follow a vegetarian diet – even if they don't want to.

Another problem for Muslims is that a ban on pork products includes not only bacon, sausages, ham, paté or salami, but also some biscuits, bread, soups, chocolate – anything that contains animal fat. Muslims have to examine every packet.

The ban against pork is shared by Jews, and Muslims think it should also be shared by Christians. They remind Christians that Isa (Jesus) never ate pork himself and left instructions that the laws of God were not to be broken.

Many Muslim children do not eat school dinners because of the food restrictions.

FOR YOUR FOLDERS

1 A Muslim wife must ensure all food eaten is halal. What does halal mean? What are the food rules for Muslims?

2 What difficulties do you think a Muslim family living in Britain might have in keeping the food laws?

3 On what grounds do Muslims argue that halal killing is not cruel?

FOR DISCUSSION

People shouldn't eat meat if they are not prepared to be responsible for killing in the kindest way.

Brechin High School

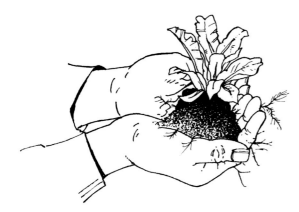

God has made you custodians of the Earth

RESPONSIBILITY

> It is He who has made you custodians (khalifas), inheritors of the Earth.
>
> (surah 6:165)

Muslims believe that Allah gave the planet to human beings for them to look after and to be its guardians. They must not pollute or damage it. On the Day of Judgement God will ask how Muslims have faced their responsibility towards the Earth, the creatures on it and the natural resources that Allah gave them to use.

Scientists have discovered how human activity affects the atmosphere and climate. For example, the greenhouse effect is caused when CFC gases damage the ozone layer and extra carbon dioxide in the atmosphere causes the planet to heat up. Industry takes resources from the earth, and then dumps waste products thoughtlessly. Other companies pollute the seas and atmosphere with the massive use of herbicides and pesticides.

Muslim scientists think that people who do not accept that they are Allah's guardians of the planet do not care about the damage they are doing.

Muslims believe God created this planet out of love, and it should be maintained through love. Muslims want to live at peace with nature and to maintain its goodness.

COMPASSION

Islam teaches that Allah loves everything He has made, so mercy and compassion are to be shown to every living creature. Islam forbids cruelty to animals.

> A student of religion saw a dog, weak with hunger. He sold his books to buy food for the dog. That night he had a dream. 'You don't need to work so hard to learn about religion, my son. We have bestowed knowledge upon you.'
>
> (adapted from a story in *Muslim Voice*, January 1990)

BLOOD SPORTS

The Prophet forbade any 'sport' that involved making animals fight each other. In the same way, Islam forbids modern blood sports such as fox-hunting, badger- bear- or dog-baiting or cock-fighting.

HUNTING

Islam teaches that no one should hunt for sport. People may only take the life of animals for food or another useful purpose.

> If someone kills a sparrow for sport, the sparrow will cry out on the Day of Judgement, 'O Lord! That person…did not kill me for any useful purpose!'
>
> (Hadith)

An animal or bird that is a natural predator cannot be blamed for doing what comes naturally to it. All hunting should be for food, and any animal used for hunting should be well trained, kept under control and not allowed to be clumsy or savage.

Weapons used for hunting should be a spear, arrow or bullet. Weapons used to club or throttle are forbidden. The idea of people clubbing seal pups for their fur is disgusting to Muslims as well as to many other people.

ANIMAL EXPERIMENTS

Scientists carry out experiments on animals for many reasons. Some of them are for the real benefit of humanity. They help to bring about progress in medicine and health. Others test reactions to substances such as cosmetics, or even to cigarettes.

Muslims believe that doing any experiment on animals just to help develop luxury goods is wrong. Most Muslims always try to find out if the things they buy have been produced using only halal (permitted) methods that are not cruel to other living things.

If there were no alternative to an experiment on an animal for medical purposes, Muslims might accept it.

ANIMALS IN CONFINEMENT

Muslims, like other caring people, believe it is wrong to keep any animal tied up, in dirty conditions or in a small space just for convenience. They believe that people who treat animals and birds like this will answer for their actions on the Day of Judgement.

Killing for luxury goods is forbidden

GREEN HADITHS OF THE PROPHET MUHAMMAD

The Earth is green and beautiful, and Allah has appointed you his stewards over it.

The whole Earth has been created a place of worship, pure and clean.

If a Muslim plants a tree or sows a field …, all of it is love on his part.

FOR DISCUSSION

- How do you think Muslims would react to factory farming and zoos?

- What do you feel about this issue?

FOR YOUR FOLDERS

1 In what ways are Muslims expected to be responsible in the way they use the planet in everyday life?

2 Write a letter to a company that you find is only interested in making a profit and not in taking care of the planet.

3 How would Muslims react to:

   a using aerosols containing CFC gases

   b buying products obtained from rare and endangered species (e.g. fur, ivory)

   c excessive use of paper and packaging

   d using non-biodegradable products (things that do not rot naturally).

SCHOOL

School problems fall into four main areas:

- school uniform, particularly PE kit
- mixed classes after age ten
- sex education in the classroom
- religious education that is Bible-based, or Islam taught in an incorrect manner.

Muslims consider that:

- girls should not wear short skirts – school uniform should allow trousers and they should wear tracksuits for PE
- girls and boys should be educated separately as soon as they begin to develop sexually, to protect them and make them concentrate on lessons
- communal showers are immodest and should not be forced on girls or boys
- sex education should only be taught by people who agree with Muslim morality.

RELIGIOUS EDUCATION

Muslims do not approve of RE teachers who:

- have no religious belief themselves
- regard Muslims as non-believers and try to convert them to Christianity
- think all religions are equal.

Muslims do not take part in school worship as they do not pray to Jesus (Isa) or in Jesus' name. They do not take part in preparations for Christmas and Easter.

PRAYER

Many employers do not provide a time or place for Muslims to pray, or a wash-room for them to wash first.

Muslim children pray at Islamia School, Brent

Although prayer times are flexible, and can follow the normal breaks in the working or school day, it is not always possible to find a suitable place. In Muslim countries people can pray anywhere, while life goes on around them.

Muslim men need time off to go to the mosque on Friday, so they usually go at lunchtime. It is helpful where they can work flexi-time to fit this in. Older boys should go too, so some may miss school lessons before or after lunch.

RAMADAN

Fasting makes some people bad-tempered, or light-headed. Many feel sick or faint, and most feel very tired in the afternoons. Some find that at night they cannot eat even when they are allowed. They become quite weak by the end of the 30 days (see unit 31). It is hard for them to do heavy physical work.

Teachers may tell pupils off for being sleepy, not realizing that some of them are hungry and may have been up until 3 a.m. with the family the night before.

In Muslim countries, school and office hours are rearranged to take account of Ramadan.

MEDICAL TREATMENT

Muslims believe it is improper for a woman to be examined by a male doctor, or a man to be examined by a female doctor. In a group practice this is no problem as usually patients can choose their doctor.

Problems arise when a Muslim has to go to hospital, or dies in hospital. Muslims find hospital rules difficult. They expect to be with their relatives when they die, and to take them away immediately for washing, prayers and burial.

DOGS

Many non-Muslims keep dogs in their houses and are pleased if they greet guests as a sign of affection. Muslims do not *dislike* dogs but they are thought of as ritually unclean animals (they are 'impure'). If a dog touches Muslims before prayers they have to change their clothes as well as doing the ritual wash.

FOR YOUR FOLDERS

1 What difficulties are there for a Muslim girl in a Western school if she keeps Shari'ah (see unit 40)?

2 Should Muslim girls give up their customs and adopt Western ways? Give reasons for your answer.

FOR DISCUSSION

'Living according to Shari'ah makes it impossible for Muslims to mix socially with non-Muslims.' Do you agree? Give reasons for your opinion.

THINGS TO DO

1 Imagine you are a Muslim parent. Write a letter to the head teacher of your daughter's school. In it, explain the problems she is facing because she is a Muslim.

2 Draw small pictures to show some of the things a Muslim who has recently arrived in Britain might find strange – the weather, food, shops, the people in your area. Write a suitable caption under each one.

'The best of you are those who are kind to your family' (Hadith)

THE BASIS OF SOCIETY

Muslims believe that God intended the family to be the basis for the human race (see surah 4:1). It should provide a secure environment for the growth and development of all its members. Nothing should weaken or threaten the family.

THE EXTENDED FAMILY

Any family is very complicated and includes many people. It is not just a husband and wife, grandparents and children. It includes brothers and sisters, uncles and aunts, and cousins. It should be a loving unit that includes neighbours and friends and anyone who needs help (see surah 2:83).

> Those who show the most perfect faith are those who possess the best [nature] and are kindest to their families.

> May his nose be rubbed in dust who found his parents approaching old age and did not enter Paradise by serving them.

(Hadiths)

RESPECT FOR SENIOR RELATIVES

In Muslim families grandparents take priority over children, who are taught to be respectful and considerate. This is because the old people of today were the workers and providers of yesterday.

As people become old they may become confused or bad tempered, or suffer from physical disabilities of old age. They may think they are *always* right, and *always* superior to their children, even when their children are in their sixties! Muslims understand all this and treat their elders with respect and compassion.

> Your Lord orders that you...be kind to parents. If one or both of them attain old age with you, do not say one word of contempt to them,...but speak to them in terms of honour...and say, My Lord, bestow your mercy on them, as they cherished me when I was a child.

(surah 17:23–4)

Muslims expect to care for their parents to the end of their days, and not hand them over to strangers in a nursing home.

RECOMMENDED RULES FOR BRINGING UP CHILDREN

- Don't take chances because of your love for them: be on your guard against misdeeds.

- Make sure they have a good education that will also prepare them to earn a living.

- Help them to make a happy marriage.

- Always be just and fair, and show them your love.

- Don't be overprotective on the one hand or careless on the other.

- Don't expect too much of them or be disappointed with their achievements.

- Accept their gifts with gratitude.

- Train them in Muslim worship. They can begin learning prayer and fasting by the age of seven.

> He who has no compassion for our little ones, and does not acknowledge the honour due to our elders, is not one of us.
>
> (Hadith)

No one child should be made the favourite in a family. Everyone should be treated equally.

> Do not ask me to be a witness to injustice. Your children have the right to receive equal treatment, as you have the right that they should honour you.
>
> Fear Allah, and treat your children with equal justice.
>
> (Hadiths)

'MILK' BROTHERS AND SISTERS

If a baby's mother dies, and the baby is given to another woman to breastfeed, that child would be regarded as a brother or sister to the woman's own children, and future marriage between them would be forbidden.

ADOPTION

The Qur'an teaches that any orphaned or abandoned children should be looked after. They should be given shelter, food, clothing and anything else they need. But there is *no* legal adoption in Islam. Muslims are forbidden to adopt a child, or to make a child from another person's family equal to their own sons and daughters.

'Adopted' children should never be misled about their true parents. They should not have the same rights as the children born into a family. This is because Muslims feel that contracts cannot make an adoptive parent's blood flow in the veins of an adopted child, or produce family affection and loyalty, or pass on inherited characteristics.

FOR YOUR FOLDERS

1 How different is the Muslim 'extended' family from your own family?

2 What advantages might there be to living in an extended family?

3 How did the Prophet think compassion should be shown to:
   a one's own children
   b orphans?

4 How do Muslims honour the old people in the family?

THINKING POINT

Which is worse? The strain caused by lack of privacy due to overcrowding in a large family, or the strain of loneliness and depression?

The father whispers the adhan in the ear of his new-born baby

Every family should welcome the birth of a new baby as a joyful event, a 'gift from God'. Muslims often regard a large number of children as a great blessing.

The ummah – the Muslim community – welcomes the baby as soon as it is born. The head of the family takes the baby into his arms and whispers the call to prayer, the adhan, in the child's right ear and the command to rise and worship in the child's left ear. So the first word the baby hears is 'God'.

TAHNIK

In the custom of **tahnik** one of the oldest relatives rubs a small piece of sugar or honey or date on the baby's gums. This symbolizes making the baby 'sweet' – obedient and kind. Prayers for the baby and the family follow.

AQIQAH

Aqiqah is the naming ceremony which takes place when the baby is seven days old. The baby's head is shaved, and by tradition the weight of the hair, in gold or silver, is set aside for the poor. Even if the baby is bald a gift of money is still given.

NAMES

The choice of a name is important. Family names or those of the Prophet's family are usually popular. Other popular names start with 'Abd', which means 'slave', added to one of the names of God, e.g. *Abdullah*, *Abdul Rahman* ('Servant of God', 'Slave of the Merciful'). They should never be 'slave' of any human, however holy or famous.

The parents of a first-born child may change their own name, to be known by the name of the child. So, parents of a child called Husain *ibn* ('son of') Dawud would become *Abu* Husain ('father of' Husain) and *Umm* Husain ('mother of' Husain).

KHITAN

If the baby is a boy he must then be circumcised (**khitan**). This means cutting the

Turkish boy dressed for circumcision

end of the foreskin from the penis. This is done at aqiqah if the baby is well and there is no need for delay. If the baby is not well, it can be left for a few months. If it is left any longer the parents would be thought to be cruel.

In some places, Khitan takes place when the boy is between seven and ten years old. In Turkey the boy is dressed up like a little prince and the circumcision takes place at a family party. This is not the recommended way in Islam and is an ordeal for the boy.

Circumcision is healthy, especially in hot countries. It avoids discomfort and disease. It does not affect sexual relations in later life.

BISMILLAH

At the age of four, a child can have the ceremony of **bismillah**. The child must be able to recite the first lesson of the Qur'an by heart – 'In the name of God, the Compassionate, the Merciful' – and can then be taught how to pray.

FOR YOUR FOLDERS

Imagine you are a guest in a Muslim home where a baby has just been born. Write to a friend describing the events of the first week of the baby's life.

QUICK QUIZ

1 What is meant by ummah?
2 What are the first words a Muslim baby should hear?
3 What is the tahnik?
4 What happens at aqiqah?
5 What sort of name should not be given to a baby?

FOR DISCUSSION

● Why do you think Muslims start training children early in the faith?

● Why would a Muslim not choose the name Abdul Muhammad, but would be pleased to be called Abdullah?

THINGS TO DO

1 Look at the picture of the Turkish boy. Why is he dressed like this? What will soon happen to him? Why?
2 Why do most Muslims have their boys circumcised soon after birth?

Muslim bride

Muslims take marriage very seriously. Muslims may marry cousins, but it is more usual for two completely separate family units to be joined by the marriage. In either case, it is thought preferable that the new husband or wife is someone whose character and background are well known.

Muslims should choose their partners with care and remain loyal to them for the rest of their lives. In due course, 'if God wills', the girl will become a mother, and the young man a father.

ARRANGED MARRIAGES

In the West, most young people think it is natural to meet someone, fall in love and then marry that person. Muslims think that 'being under the influence of love' can be dangerous and can cloud the judgement. For this reason Muslim parents often arrange marriages for their children. They will always try to find good, compatible partners – and they may not approve of an unwise romance.

However, forced marriages are forbidden in Islam. Marriage must be with the consent of both partners, and they have the right to disagree with their parents' choice.

MAHR (DOWRY)

The **mahr** or dowry is a sum of money paid by the husband to the wife. It does not have to be a lot, but it is the wife's right to keep it if she is later divorced. If she divorces her husband against his will, she must return the mahr.

It is against the Prophet's way of life to demand high dowries, or not to give a dowry at all. It should not be paid to the bride's father as compensation for the loss of his daughter – though this may happen in some cultures.

THE WEDDING – NIKAH

The ceremony is quite simple, consisting of readings from the Qur'an, the exchange of vows in front of witnesses, and prayers. No special religious official need be present, though often the imam attends this happy event. Even the bride need not go, as long as she sends her wali or representative and two witnesses to confirm her agreement.

The **nikah** (wedding) contract may be signed before the actual wedding – sometimes years before. Nikah is not a sacred contract 'made in heaven' but is like a business contract giving husband and wife rights and responsibilities.

A sensible bride includes in the contract conditions that could help her if she later needed to start divorce proceedings. For example, she could make it clear that she does not give permission for her husband to have a second wife.

WALIMA

The **walima** is the celebration party after the wedding and usually follows within three days of the couple starting to live together. Presents are given, usually of money. Some people hold huge, expensive parties, but this has nothing to do with Islam. The Prophet disapproved of lavish show, especially if it caused hardship to the bride or groom or their families.

It is considered impolite not to attend the walima if you are invited.

COUSIN MARRIAGES

Many Muslims seem to marry their cousins. Where this is common, it can cause distress if birth defects occur in children. It also makes it hard for a couple to divorce if other close relations will be offended.

MONEY MATTERS

Cooking and cleaning are not part of a wife's duties. She is to supervise the household. So the husband should provide her with a helper if he can afford it. If he cannot afford it, or the wife enjoys housework, it is counted an act of charity on her part.

Muslim women keep any property they owned before marriage, and any salary they earn if they go out to work. They need not share them with their husbands. They need not change their name on marriage.

MIXED MARRIAGES

Muslim boys may marry Christians or Jews. They may only marry Hindu, Buddhist or Sikh girls if the brides convert to Islam. Muslim girls are not allowed to marry non-Muslims. In Islam the children take the religion of the father.

THE RIGHT TO COMPATIBILITY IN MARRIAGE

> The Prophet said, 'A woman should only be married to a person who is good enough for her or compatible to her.'
>
> (Hadith)

The only compatibility that matters in a Muslim marriage is piety.

> Do not marry only for a person's looks; ...Do not marry for wealth,...Marry rather on the grounds of religious devotion.
>
> (Hadith)

In marriage the partner should be like a best friend – someone who shares the difficulties of life as well as its pleasures.

FOR YOUR FOLDERS

1 Why do Muslims think that marrying 'under the influence of love' is dangerous?

2 Explain the meaning of mahr, nikah and walima.

3 What advantages are there for the wife in a Muslim marriage?

4 What makes an ideal bride or husband (for anyone, not just Muslims)?

TALKING POINTS

- Does the arranged marriage system have advantages for the young couple? Explain your answer.

- How important is it for a person to marry someone who shares their religious beliefs?

Brechin High School

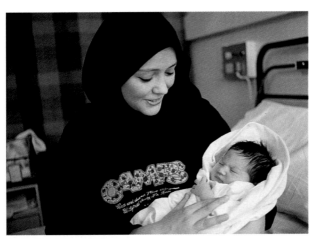

Islam stresses the importance of motherhood

MOTHER

A loving and secure household does not just happen by chance. Everyone has to work at it with commitment, patience, forgiveness, tolerance and a sense of duty and love.

All these qualities are vital, and the person at the centre of the family and who does most of the work is the mother.

Muslims consider a good mother to be a precious treasure. When a woman becomes a mother she takes on responsibility for her children's human rights:

- the right to life, and equal chances in life

- the right to a name – which means every child should legally have a father

- the right to a good and loving upbringing.

THE TEAM

A Muslim mother takes responsibility for:

- food for the hungry

- refuge for the weary

- hospitality for the guest

- comfort for the distressed

- peace for the troubled

- hope for the insecure

- encouragement for the weak.

The father should protect and provide for the household. He makes it possible for the mother to fulfil her role.

It is the father's responsibility to bring in money, and his duty to be honourable and earn respect. The father's role involves not only his job, but also leadership, responsibility and duty to his family.

PARTNERSHIP IN MARRIAGE

In Islam, marriage is a partnership. Muslim women accept Allah as their master and do not consider themselves to be inferior to their husbands. In Muslim society the man is responsible for taking care of his family outside the home, but the woman rules within the household.

Every institution works best if there is a clear leader. Most Muslim women are quite happy for the leader within the family to be the man they love. If the man is not worth respecting, divorce is quite straightforward and she may look for a better man. If the woman is more intelligent or practical than the man, he will sensibly leave most things to her. However, in Islam he is still *responsible* for her.

THE HUSBAND'S RIGHTS

Husbands have the right to:

- a sexual relationship – husbands and wives should not refuse each other

- discretion – the couple's sex lives, problems and family matters are private

- obedience, except if the husband goes against Islam – wives may not mix with people the husband disapproves of or go where he does not wish, and if there is a difference of opinion, the husband's decision must be accepted, for better or worse

- faithfulness – if the wife is unfaithful, the husband is allowed to chastise (strike) his wife as a last resort; if that fails, the marriage has failed.

The best of treasures is a good wife. She is pleasing in her husband's eyes, looks for ways to please him, and takes care of his possessions while he is away; the best of you are those who treat their wives best.

(Hadith)

THE RIGHT TO BE PROTECTED

Men are the protectors and maintainers of women, because Allah has given them more [strength]

(surah 4:34)

Islam accepts that women are equal to men. However it takes account of the physical differences between the sexes.

A Muslim woman has the right to remain a virgin and not to be pestered by strangers or male members of her own family. She has the right to enter marriage a virgin, and to give herself to her chosen partner for life. She has the right to be cared for when ill or in pain, for example during her monthly periods, through pregnancy and while raising children.

While women are allowed to work, they should not be forced to work. A Muslim woman has the right to be looked after by her husband if she does not wish to go out to work. She has the right to work without sexual harassment at the workplace.

The Prophet was never chauvinistic or sexist. He helped his wives in the home, mended his own clothes and shoes, made up his own bed and so on. Where a Muslim's wife goes out to work, it is good manners for him to help in the home and share the duties in the evenings, as the Prophet did.

FOR YOUR FOLDERS

1 How are Muslim men expected to behave:

   a in the home (towards the family)

   b at work (as employer or employee)

   c in society (as a responsible citizen)?

2 Should a woman be obedient to her husband? Are there circumstances when a Muslim woman might not be obedient to her husband? Give reasons for your answer.

3 Write two lists: 'A husband's rights and responsibilities' and 'A wife's rights and responsibilities'.

4 Why do you think the Prophet put so much value on the mother of a family? (See Hadith in Thinking Point, below.)

THINKING POINT

A man asked the Prophet, 'Who…is most worthy of my company?' The Prophet replied, 'Your mother.' The man asked, 'Who next?' The Prophet said, 'Your mother.' The man again asked, 'Who next?' Again the Prophet said, 'Your mother.' Only next did he say 'Your father.'

(Hadith)

POLYGAMY

> Marry women of your choice, two or three or four; but if you fear you will not be able to deal justly with them, then only one.

> You will never be able to be fair and just between women…

(surah 4:3 and 129)

Polygamy means having more than one husband or wife. When men have more than one wife the proper term is polygyny. The two quotes above show that monogamy (having only one partner) is the ideal for a Muslim family. However, a Muslim man is allowed to have more than one wife. Islam did not introduce this system. Polygamy already existed in many cultures in ancient times. True polygamy (men *or* women having more than one wife or husband) is not allowed in Islam.

The Prophet Muhammad had twelve wives after the death of his first wife Khadijah. Then Allah revealed to him that Muslim men were allowed up to four wives, provided that:

● the first wife gave her permission

● later wives were not a cause of distress

● all wives would be treated equally, i.e. given the same quality and amount of food, clothing, health care, leisure, living space, time, compassion and mercy.

Making love equally is not required, but sharing time equally is.

If a man takes a new wife for the wrong reasons, that marriage could be declared illegal. It is against the principles of Islam. A man is not supposed to satisfy his lust by trading in an old wife for a younger model!

POLYANDRY

Polyandry means a woman has more than one husband at one time. Islam is against

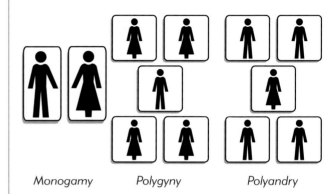

Monogamy   Polygyny   Polyandry

polyandry because a child has the right to know who their father is. This would not always be possible if the woman was married to more than one man.

SOCIAL REASONS FOR POLYGAMY

In a society where there are more women than men, strict monogamy would mean that many women would have no chance of marriage. A widow or divorcee might prefer to be a second wife rather than be lonely. Even so, a man should not cause his existing wife to be upset.

Wives could become mentally or physically ill and unable to perform their wifely functions. This could result in a husband having to control his instincts for the rest of his life, or to take a mistress or to divorce his first wife. Muslims think any of these would be unreasonable. A second wife could be a second mother to his children, help run the household and help the husband to take care of the first wife.

Some older wives welcome a younger wife. She may be a good worker and have modern training, for example as a nurse.

DISADVANTAGES OF POLYGAMY

The four disadvantages of polygamy are jealousy, inequality, arguments among the wives and conflicts between the children of different wives. These must all be taken into

Demonstrating birth control in a women's health clinic, Cairo

account when considering a polygamous marriage.

> The rights of a woman are sacred; ensure that women are maintained in the rights assigned to them.

(Hadith)

EQUALITY

> All people are equal…as the teeth of a comb. No Arab can claim merit over a non-Arab, nor a white over a black person, nor a male over a female.

(Hadith)

Throughout history women have suffered because power has been in the hands of men. Women have frequently been treated as servants and the property of men.

The Qur'an teaches that men and women are different, but are of equal worth. Every instruction in the Qur'an applies to male and female believers. The Prophet made it clear that 'Man' meant all humanity and not just the male sex. Both sexes have the same religious duties and will be judged in the same way.

EMPOWERING WOMEN

Muslims believe that men are natural leaders. However, many talented women become able teachers and administrators. Muslims who object to this often quote the Prophet's wry comment, that misfortunes will always arise when women are in charge. This was not an order or a ruling. Indeed the Qur'an gives the example of the Queen of Sheba who became Muslim but was asked not to give up her throne (surah 27:31, 42–4).

In the 1990s, three of the world's prime ministers were Muslim women: Benazir Bhutto of Pakistan, Kaleda Zia of Bangladesh and Tanzu Ciller of Turkey.

Many Muslim women scholars work for the improvement of conditions for women in backward societies. They hope to change the way that Islamic law has been abused by extremist Muslim men who do not apply the true principles of Islam (see unit 69).

TALKING POINT

What do you think that 'equality in marriage' means? Can women claim to be equal if they are denied the same rights as men in marriage?

FOR YOUR FOLDERS

1 Make a list of the conditions under which a Muslim man might take more than one wife.

2 How might a Muslim woman answer a critic who said that in Islam women are inferior to men?

Not every marriage is successful

Either keep your wife honestly, or put her away from you with kindness. Do not force a woman to stay with you who wishes to leave.

(surah 2:231)

Islam discourages divorce, but allows it so that people do not have to suffer a life of misery.

If a wife fears cruelty or desertion on her husband's part, there is no blame on them if they arrange an amicable settlement between themselves.

(surah 4:128)

The most detestable act that God has permitted is divorce.

(Hadith)

Muslims believe that divorce is the last resort after all attempts to put things right have failed.

DIVORCE BY MUTUAL CONSENT

- **Mubara'ah** – the husband and wife agree to the divorce and work out the finances between them.

- **Khul** – A wife can divorce her husband if she has a good reason. She must return the dowry in exchange for the divorce (see unit 49). She has the right to keep the dowry if her husband divorces her.

CONDITIONS NECESSARY FOR THE DIVORCE TO BE VALID

- The partners must be sane and of a clear mind, and not under pressure from outside parties.

- The reasons for the divorce must be clear.

- The partners must not be under the influence of alcohol or drugs. They must not be so angry that they do not know what they are doing.

GROUNDS FOR A WIFE TO DIVORCE HER HUSBAND

- The husband is unable or refuses to maintain her.

- Abuse or ill treatment.

- The husband is impotent (cannot have sex).

- The husband has an incurable, repulsive disease or is mentally ill.

- The husband is absent and has not communicated (desertion).

- The husband is in prison.

- The husband has concealed important information or deceived his wife when making the marriage contract.

TALAQ AND IDDAH

Talaq is a divorce requested by the husband.

Islam requires the husband to be honourable and decent. The husband has to pronounce his intention to divorce three times. Then there must be a waiting time or **iddah** before the divorce becomes final. This is usually three months. If the wife is pregnant it has to be nine months. During iddah the wife can continue to live in the family home. She is entitled to full maintenance and must be treated well. This is a time for both partners to think again.

If the couple make up their differences during the iddah, they do not have to remarry. After the iddah, the couple can remarry with a new contract. They are allowed remarriage a second and third time.

However, if a wife has been divorced and remarried the same husband twice, they are not allowed a third remarriage until the woman has been married to some other person. This marriage must last at least a month.

After the waiting time no one can prevent the woman from marrying whoever she chooses.

> Do not prevent them from marrying their [former] husbands if they agree among themselves in an honourable manner.
>
> (surah 2:232)

LI'AN

This is a divorce where the wife is accused of adultery. This has to be proved by four eye-witnesses. If this proof is not available, the husband can swear four times he is telling the truth. The wife then has to swear her innocence. The marriage is usually reckoned to be beyond repair and divorce is allowed.

RELUCTANTLY ALLOWED

Divorce *must* be allowed when the marriage has completely broken down; it is *recommended* when the wife is not fulfilling her obligations; it is *disapproved* of but *reluctantly allowed* if harm might come about by continuing the marriage; and it is left to the conscience of the couple when there would be a chance of reconciliation. Divorce is haram during the wife's monthly periods.

CUSTODY OF CHILDREN

A mother has custody of any small children provided she is fit to raise them and she has not remarried. The father is responsible for the financial upkeep of the children. Children who are old enough to express themselves will have their wishes taken into account.

In some societies, when the divorce is the fault of the husband he has to pay the woman's living expenses for one year.

THINKING POINT

Why is it a serious matter for a woman to be divorced by her husband in Muslim society?

FOR DISCUSSION

Many Muslims think it is better for couples to stick together no matter what is going on. Why do you think so many Muslims are set against divorce?

FOR YOUR FOLDERS

1 How do Islamic principles of marriage and divorce compare with what you know of others in the West?

2 Why do you think Muslims regard children of broken marriages as the responsibility of the father?

The final goal is to your Lord. It is He who causes both laughter and grief; it is He who causes people to die and to be born; it is He who caused male and female; it is He who will re-create us anew.

(surah 53:42–7)

When a person dies their deeds come to an end except in respect of three matters which are left behind: a continuing charity, knowledge which still brings benefit, and righteous offspring to pray for them.

(Hadith)

'Righteous offspring' means 'good children'.

It is natural for people to feel deep sorrow and pain when someone they love dies. They feel a terrible sense of loss. They wonder how on earth they will be able to go on without their loved one.

However, if Muslims have lived according to Shari'ah they hope to accept the passing calmly. This is because they have been preparing for this day from the moment of birth.

Some people do not care about life after death. Some do not believe in it at all. Muslims are certain that all humans belong to God and will return to Him. They do not see death as the end of life. Rather, this is a time when a person leaves the earthly family to go to be close to God.

Muslims believe that we should all care about life after death, since we know that all humans die.

Does Man think that We shall not assemble his bones? Yes, surely, yes – We are able to restore even his finger-tips.

(surah 75:3–4)

A Muslim headstone, Hull Cemetery

THE LAST WORD

When a Muslim knows death is close, friends and relatives come and gather round the bed. The person who is dying asks for forgiveness and blessing from loved ones and from God. Muslims hope that the last word they hear will be 'God'.

THE WAITING

Muslims believe the soul waits in barzakh (the Waiting Place) until the Day of Judgement (see unit 20). On this day God will deal with everyone, living and dead. Judgement Day, or the Day of Resurrection, may not come for hundreds of years. Unlike Earth time, this will pass in a flash – for those waiting in barsakh are outside time.

THE FINAL SALAH

Grief is normal but Muslims believe too much screaming and weeping shows lack of faith.

As soon as possible after death, the body is washed all over. This takes place at the mosque, at a special Muslim building or at home. Then scents and spices are used to anoint the body, which is wrapped in a shroud made of sheets of white cloth, three for a man and five for a woman.

The funeral prayers, called **Salat-ul-Janaza** are the usual salah words but with no prostrations to earth. There are extra prayers for forgiveness.

THE FUNERAL

Funerals are simple and not expensive. It is forbidden to have elaborate or costly funerals. In death there is no rich or poor, important or humble. Everyone is the same. There is no class system for the dead, and so there are no special cemeteries for important or rich people – nor do they have expensive tombstones.

It is sunnah for Muslims to be buried in the earth and not cremated. They do not use coffins except when it is necessary for health reasons, as they prefer to bury the body straight in the earth. They also prefer to carry the body to the cemetery, not to take it in a vehicle. Muslims believe that walking is more respectful than riding in comfort.

Muslims turn the face of the dead person to the right, and bury them so they face Makkah. They also only allow one body per grave. For these reasons, it is better to have a separate Muslim cemetery or a special section in a town cemetery. This avoids problems for other religions, or local authorities.

As they lower the body into the grave they say:

> In the name of God we commit you to the earth, according to the Way of the Prophet of God.

Then they sprinkle a little earth in the grave and say:

> We created you from it, and We return you into it, and from it We will raise you a second time.

(surah 20:55)

Mourning lasts for three days, but widows may mourn for four months and ten days. They should not re-marry during this period.

The relatives pay off any debts owed by the one who has died. They support the bereaved until they are sure they can cope again.

FOR YOUR FOLDERS

1 Why do Muslims think that it is not good to show too much grief at a funeral, or to pay for an expensive tombstone?

2 How are dead Muslims best honoured and remembered?

THINGS TO DO

1 Imagine you are invited to the funeral of a Muslim boy. Describe what happens from the moment he dies until his burial.

2 Copy one of the prayers or passages from the Qur'an or Hadiths. What do you think it means?

TALKING POINT

Only a few local authorities in Britain provide for Muslims burials. Should Muslims accept local customs, and give up their own funeral traditions?

A man prays in the desert

A mosque is a building used for Muslim worship. The name in Arabic is *masjid*, which means 'a place where people prostrate themselves'. This is where they bow and touch their heads to the earth as a sign of their humility before God.

Some mosques are very grand, like the ones at Makkah, Madinah, Jerusalem, Damascus, Cairo, Istanbul and the one in Regent's Park in London. There are pictures of these fine buildings on this page and pages 111, 112 and 113.

Other mosques may not be noticed by non-Muslims. A mosque can be anywhere that people choose to worship God and perform salah. In Muslim countries they may be little areas marked out by roadside teashops, or in fields or at railway stations. There may be just a mat and an arrow to show the direction of Makkah.

In Britain Muslims have converted all sorts of buildings to be used as mosques – old churches, houses, even a fire station.

As Muhammad said:

> Wherever the hour of prayer overtakes you, you shall perform it. That place is a mosque.

(Hadith)

The place does not matter. The Qur'an says:

> …God knows everything in the heavens and on earth. Three men cannot talk together in secret, but He is the fourth… Neither fewer than that or more, but He is with them, wherever they may be.

(surah 58:7)

Many Muslims keep a spare room, or a part of a bedroom so that there is always a clean, suitable place. This allows them to shut out the cares of the world from their minds, and come before God in prayer.

The Prophet's family home in Madinah consisted of several small mud-brick huts for the Prophet and his wives set around a square courtyard. There was a palm-leafed roof for shade. This was the first mosque.

King Faisal Mosque, Islamabad, Pakistan

The Badshahi Mosque,
Lahore, Pakistan

The Blue Mosque,
near Kuala Lumpur, Malaysia

Jamia Mosque, Nairobi, Kenya

Shir-Dah Madrasah and Mosque,
Samarkand, Uzbekistan

FOR YOUR FOLDERS

1 Is it important for a religious group to have a special place where they can meet? Give reasons for your answer.

2 Copy out surah 58:7. What does this teach about the presence of God?

FOR DISCUSSION

- God can be worshipped anywhere. The most important place of worship is the heart.

- Splendid buildings are a waste of money and effort.

Regent's Park Mosque, London

Before entering the Mosque, Muslims take off their shoes and perform wudu (see unit 25). There is usually a well, fountain or tap in the courtyard, or a special washroom in a modern building. Most modern mosques provide a separate washroom for women.

Worshippers leave their shoes on a rack outside the prayer room. When the congregation is very large, they take their shoes with them, in a bag, to avoid a frantic scramble after the service.

The prayer room feels very spacious and airy. This is because there are no chairs or other furniture. Everyone sits or kneels on the floor, which is covered with carpets.

There is often a design on the carpet or lines to help the believers to form neat rows. There may be little individual mats, all placed pointing to Makkah.

The dome in the roof represents the universe and adds to the sense of space. It also helps the voice of the imam to be heard clearly.

Inside Regent's Park Mosque

MIHRABS

The mihrab is a niche set in the wall that faces Makkah. Mihrabs are often beautifully decorated with coloured tiles and texts from the Qur'an. They are sometimes called the 'niche of lights' and symbolize the presence of God in the hearts of believers.

Many mihrabs are shell-shaped. This is to give the idea that they house a 'pearl of great price'. It is important that the most elaborate decoration is used to honour something that is not itself visible.

Mihrab, Cairo Mosque, Egypt

Minbar, Cairo, Egypt

NO PICTURES

There are no pictures or statues in a mosque as it is forbidden to make images of God or spiritual beings. Muslims believe this is an insult to God. Images of the Prophet are also forbidden.

However, mosques are far from dull. There are carpets in rich colours, brightly patterned tiles, marble pillars, crystal chandeliers, carved stonework and stained-glass windows.

There is a **minbar** or pulpit from which sermons are given. It may be very ornate or just a platform at the top of a few steps.

In modern mosques, men and women have separate entrances and separate rooms for worship.

There is sometimes a mortuary for preparing dead Muslims for burial.

Decorative tiles, Isfahan, Iran

A **minaret** is a tower from which the call to prayer is given (see the picture on page 51). Some mosques have more than one minaret. There may be a large walled courtyard. One wall is higher than the others and has a huge archway in it. This is the qiblah wall, which marks the direction of Makkah.

THINGS TO DO

Write an interview with a Muslim guide at the mosque. These are the questions to put to him. Write your own answers to the questions using the information in this unit.

1 What does the qiblah show?

2 What is a minaret used for?

3 Why do mosques need a water supply?

4 What do Muslims do as they enter a mosque?

5 Why are there no pictures or statues?

6 Why are there lines or a pattern on the carpet?

FOR YOUR FOLDERS

1 Use a computer graphics package or your own artistic skills to produce a decorative panel for a mosque, using ideas from this unit.

2 In what ways do you think the design of a mosque helps Muslims to concentrate on their prayers?

Children learning at the mosque school

USES

The Prophet did not separate religious life from normal daily activities. In the courtyard he met visitors, conducted business and held political meetings. It was also where he sheltered the homeless poor and cared for the sick. It was the place where believers met for prayer and to hear his sermons.

The well in the courtyard was not only for washing before prayers, but also for drinking. Travellers were given refreshment and visitors could stay there overnight.

Today mosques are still used for all these functions. In places where Muslims are in a minority it is very important for them to have a place to meet and discuss their problems.

Mosques are also used:

- as schools – for learning Arabic and studying the Qur'an
- as law courts – for Islamic law
- for celebrations of births, marriages and deaths
- for parties, lectures and social activities.

BEHAVIOUR

People should behave quietly and show respect at all times, not just at prayer times.

People can relax and students of all ages – even very old people – can be seen there studying, reading, taking a nap or playing table-tennis in the community room.

SCHOOL

Most mosques have a **madrasah**. This is a school where Muslims do their 'Islamiat' or Islamic studies. In Britain this is from 4 p.m. until 6 p.m., five nights a week, and sometimes even at weekends.

In Muslim countries, children do Islamiat during the day as part of normal lessons. They think this is the most important part of their education.

Children begin Islamic studies when they are five. Girls continue until the age of twelve, and boys go on until age fifteen. Students may spend the rest of their lives in study, and may become teachers themselves. Muslims who are not Arabs must learn Arabic to study

A social gathering at the Mosque

the Qur'an properly. Good students learn portions of the Qur'an by heart. Some learn it all and become hafiz (see unit 21).

There is an exam every year and most children pass it. They all change classes after Ramadan. Most teachers are not specially trained but are unpaid volunteers. They are allowed to use the cane, but they rarely do, because the children are polite and respectful towards their elders.

FOR YOUR FOLDERS

1 Describe some of the social activities that take place at the mosque building. How do these help to strengthen the feeling of ummah (community)?

2 What happens at the madrasah?

3 Why is it hard for young Muslims to study Islamiat in:

   a non-Arabic countries

   b non-Muslim countries?

4 Why is it important for a Muslim to learn to read Arabic?

THINKING POINT

Does the use of the mosque for purposes other than prayer prevent it from being a 'holy' place?

FOR DISCUSSION

God does not exist in one place alone. Why do you think that some people believe that they can come closer to God in certain places?

Brechin High School

Virtue is goodness or living a good life. For Muslims it is not enough simply to believe in God and life after death. They must show their faith in action (amal, see unit 23). This means trying to be as God would want them to be.

Muslims believe that God is the One who created the universe. He is also our closest friend and helper. He knows our most private thoughts:

> It was We who created Man, and We know what dark suggestions his soul makes to him [i.e. our innermost desires and motives]; for We are nearer to him than his jugular vein.
>
> (surah 50:16)

Muslims believe that:

> God does not look upon your bodies and appearances; He looks upon your hearts and deeds.
>
> (Hadith)

FAITH

The chief virtue, or quality, of a Muslim is faith. This means having a deep love for God, trusting Him and living your life to please Him.

> You should worship God as if you are seeing Him; for He sees you even if you do not see Him.
>
> (Hadith)

HONESTY

A person cannot claim to love God and then lie, cheat, break promises and let others down. Therefore honesty, truthfulness, sincerity and integrity are essential aspects of being a Muslim. The Prophet said, 'Always speak the truth, even if it is bitter.'

JUSTICE

Muslim justice should not be influenced by personal friendship or wealth or status.

> O believers, be seekers after justice, witnesses for God, even though it be against yourselves or your parents and kinsmen; or whether [the person] be rich or poor, for God is the protector of both.
>
> (surah 4:135)

COMPASSION

A Muslim should be compassionate and merciful. This means being kind and caring. This is one of the qualities of God, and every surah begins 'In the name of God, the Compassionate, the Merciful One.'

People who are unkind are often unaware of their own failings, or they may have lived a very sheltered and protected life.

Muslims believe that Allah asks them to be more caring than anyone else, to give a bit extra, even to those who did not help when you were in need.

> ...give to the one who did not help you when you were in need, and keep fellowship with the one who did not care about you.
>
> (Hadith)

A Muslim should be compassionate

Muslims believe that Allah asks them to show compassion to:

- parents
- children
- one's partner in marriage
- orphans
- the sick, wounded and handicapped
- servants, helpers and employees
- animals.

> He who has no compassion for our little ones is not one of us. (Hadith)

GENEROSITY

Muslims think themselves lucky if they have enough to share with others as in this way they share Allah's love. A virtuous person…

> …gives food, for the love of Him, to the needy, the orphan, the prisoner of war [saying]: 'We feed you only for the sake of Allah; we desire no repayment from you, and no thanks.' (surah 76:7–10)

MODESTY

Muslims believe that all their talents come from Allah and that it is not right to show off. They do not seek applause or praise, but only God's approval. They dress modestly and respect people who are sexually pure.

> Modesty and faith are joined…; if either of them is lost, the other goes too. (Hadith)

TOLERANCE

Muslims believe they should respect the rights of others.

> Let there be no coercion in religion. (surah 2:256)

PATIENCE, COURAGE AND FORTITUDE

When Muslims are faced with difficulties in life they remember God and face their tests with patience, courage and strength. This is called **sabr**. They do not run away from life but hold on to their faith while trouble lasts.

> Be firm and patient in pain (or suffering) and adversity, and throughout all periods of panic. (surah 2:177)

> Muslims who live in the midst of society and bear with patience the afflictions that come to them are better than those who shun society and cannot bear any wrong done to them. (Hadith)

FOR DISCUSSION

If there is no God, and no life after death, virtuous living is a waste of time.

FOR YOUR FOLDERS

1 How could a person show courage and strength when faced with
   a divorced parents
   b redundancy from work
   c terminal illness (their own or another's)?

2 Write a list of the Muslim virtues. Describe a time when someone you know put them into practice.

3 Is virtuous living worthwhile – or a waste of time? Give reasons for your answer.

Work is important

THE IMPORTANCE OF WORK

Muslims believe that it is very important that a person works unless they are unable to work because of illness or age. They strongly disapprove of people who avoid work. Muslim men should earn enough to support their families.

While some mosques have a full-time, paid imam, this is not ideal. Any scholar of Islam could carry out this duty without being paid.

BEGGING

Muslims think it is shameful to beg or live off other people. They should be self-reliant and not depend on others except in real necessity.

> He who begs without need is like a person holding a burning coal in his hand.

> It is better that a person should take a rope and bring a bundle of wood on his back to sell so that Allah may preserve his honour, than that he should beg from people.

(Hadiths)

THE DIGNITY OF WORK

The Prophet taught that Muslims should never be snobbish. The person who is a simple porter has as much right to respect as a managing director. What counts is the person's dignity, honesty and attitude to the work being done.

Communities need people to collect their rubbish just as much as they need doctors. No one should think any useful job is beneath them. Nuh and Isa were carpenters, Musa was a shepherd and Muhammad was a trader.

Trading is worthwhile employment provided it is done honestly and does not exploit anyone. Muslims are not allowed to hoard goods in times of plenty in order to raise the prices in times of shortage.

> He who brings goods for sale is blessed with good fortune, but he who keeps them until the price rises is accursed.

(Hadith)

Any form of cheating or unfair trading is a disgrace. This includes making false statements about goods or giving short measure. The Prophet worked most of his life as an honest trader and thought very highly of them.

> On the Day of Resurrection Allah will not look at…the person who swears to the truth while lying about his merchandise.

(Hadith)

RESPONSIBILITY TO THE COMMUNITY

Muslims try to develop crafts and industries that are necessary and helpful to the community. These professions are called **fard** kifiyah, or collective obligations. Every Muslim community tries to include people in the areas of medicine, education, science and technology.

They also need politicians, community leaders and people in various industries.

Sometimes an individual's choice of work may be sacrificed if it is for the good of the community. The people as a whole come before any private interest or individual profit.

FORBIDDEN WORK

Muslims are forbidden to earn a living in any way that harms other people. This is haram. If work is fair and good then it is halal. Any work that involves dishonesty, sexual displays or taking advantage of people's weaknesses is forbidden.

Work that is forbidden includes:

- earning money through prostitution, indecency or pornography
- dance or drama that is deliberately erotic
- drawing, painting or photography designed to excite people sexually
- manufacturing or trading in alcohol or drugs
- working in a bar, off-licence, night club, etc.
- trade in pork
- running a 'black market' in scarce foods and other necessities
- immoral practices
- gambling.

(See surahs 5:90–2, 2:275 and 188, 4:2, 6:152, 7:85, 3:180, 9:34–5)

No body which has been nourished with what is unlawful will enter Paradise.

People make long prayers to Allah although their food and clothing are unlawfully acquired. How can the prayer of such people be accepted.

(Hadiths)

DUTIES

Muslims take seriously the duties of:

- employees – they should be honest and hardworking, not lazy or time-wasters
- employers – they should not exploit their workers. They should ensure that working conditions are reasonable, safe and pleasant. They should not make their employees work too many hours, or to a state of exhaustion. They should pay them a fair wage, on time.

Give the worker his wages before his sweat dries.

If that which the employer demands is necessary, the master himself should lend a helping hand to the servant.

(Hadiths)

FOR DISCUSSION

- How far do you think Muslim work ethics are reasonable today when most people seem concerned only with making money?
- What do you think the Hadiths above, in this column, mean?

THINGS TO DO

1 Make a list of ten jobs traditionally done by:

   a men   **b** women.

   Put a tick against those that you think would be acceptable to Muslims.

2 Give four examples of jobs that would be forbidden work for Muslims and say why each of them is forbidden.

Brechin High School

It is not poverty that I fear for you, but that you might begin to desire the world as others before you desired it, and it might destroy you as it destroyed them.

Riches are sweet…but they are not blessed for him who seeks them out of greed. He is like one who eats but is not filled.

(Hadiths)

Every community needs money to provide services such as schools, hospitals, roads and rubbish collection. Muslims do not think it is right for a wealthy person to spend a fortune on themselves while poor people go without.

He is not a believer who eats his fill while his neighbour remains hungry by his side.

(Hadith)

Muslims should not be extravagant or wasteful, but careful and thrifty. This does not mean they should not have any money at all, nor that they should not enjoy life. Muslims should be grateful for what they have and use it responsibly.

O believers! Make not unlawful the good things Allah has made lawful for you. But commit no excess, for Allah does not love those given to excess.

(surah 5:90)

TIMES OF NEED

For a person who suffers hardship and loses his property, it is permissible for him to ask until he can stand on his own feet.

(Hadith)

Although the Prophet disapproved of begging, sometimes there are times when people need to ask for money. National and personal disasters can occur. People need help with housing or business. They cannot be blamed if they are forced to ask for help

Moderation in all things

from the government or from individuals. This is one reason why governments need to be thrifty – so that they can help others.

MODERATION

Muslims do not approve of greed or ostentation (showing off). Islam values moderation:

- in eating and drinking – all leftovers should be re-used or fed to wildlife

- in dress – Muslims should not spend too much money on expensive clothes

- in the home – furniture and ornaments should be moderately priced and not showy; silver or gold should not be used for ornaments or utensils

- in buildings – no large sums should be spent on houses or palaces, or even on mosques

- at social functions – weddings or funerals should be modest

- in hospitality – generosity is approved of, but not if it is extravagant or at the cost of the family budget.

THE WARNING

If you possessed all the gold in the earth, you could not buy your place in the Hereafter with it.

(Hadith)

INTEREST – RIBA

One of the worst things that can happen for poor people is to fall into debt. Moneylenders may charge very high rates of interest. This is called usury or **riba**. It is worse for people who only borrow out of desperation.

Muslims are forbidden to exploit anybody in need by lending them money and charging interest. Instead, they should help the poor through charity, lending without interest.

The teaching about not exploiting the poor came through the Prophet Musa (Moses), see Exodus 22:25 and Leviticus 25:36–7. Isa (Jesus) said the same thing, 'Lend without interest, not hoping for anything back,' (Luke 6:34–4). The Qur'an repeats this teaching.

> Give what is necessary to your family, the needy and the wayfarer.
>
> (surah 30:38)

> If the debtor is in difficulty, grant him time to repay. …your repayment would actually be greater if you cancelled the debt.
>
> (surah 2:280)

In the West the system of mortgages for house purchase causes great hardship. Many do not realize that a mortgage of, say, £40 000 means a repayment of around £120 000. Islam regards this as usury (riba) and regrets any system that imposes this kind of debt.

TRADE DEALINGS

Taking huge profits in trade is seen as a form of riba.

> …those who eat usury [i.e. whose food is supplied by making profit from interest] will not stand,…They say 'usury is the same as trade'; but God has permitted trade and forbidden usury.
>
> (from surah 2:274–5, see also 3:130, 4:161)

In Islam no one should try to take advantage of another person in business, whether they are producers, traders or customers. Customers can be guilty of riba if they wait until goods have lost their value and then force the trader to agree a lower price. For example, fruit will only stay fresh for a limited time. On the other hand, hoarding by traders in time of shortage is condemned.

Muslims believe in using all resources that are available, including unemployed people, unused land, water and mineral resources.

FOR DISCUSSION

- Richness does not lie in abundance of worldly goods, but true richness is the richness of the soul.

- For every nation and Ummah there is a temptation or test, and the test for my Ummah is wealth.

  (Hadiths)

FOR YOUR FOLDERS

1 Explain what Muslims mean by extravagance, moderation and riba.

2 Why might it be harder for a wealthy person than for a poor one to be a true Muslim? Support your answer with quotes from the Hadiths.

3 In what ways can a Muslim show moderation?

4 Why do Muslims disapprove of those who lend money at interest?

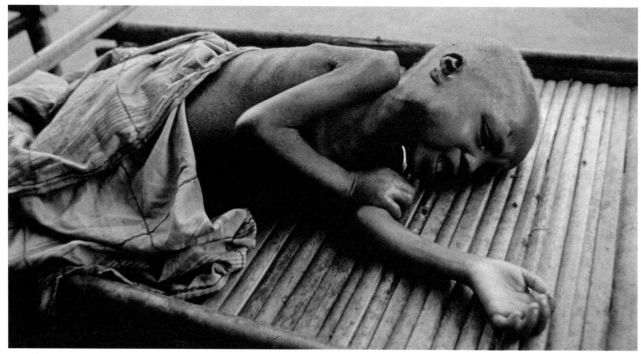

Famine in Africa

If anyone supplies a need to any one of my people, desiring to please him by it, he has pleased me; and he who has pleased me has pleased Allah; and he who has pleased Allah will be brought to Paradise.

(Hadith)

Muslims believe they can show their love for God by loving and caring for others. Muslim parents often tell their children these words of the Prophet to encourage giving:

Every day two angels come down from Heaven, one of them says, 'O Allah! Reward every person who gives in Your name.' The other says, 'O Allah! Destroy every miser!'

(Hadith)

ZAKAH AND SADAQAH

There are two kinds of giving for charity. The first is zakah (see unit 30). This is a kind of tax on a Muslim's wealth and income and is a religious duty.

When Muslims give as a matter of choice, and not duty, this is called sadaqah. The amounts may be small, perhaps individual gifts after hearing about someone in trouble.

Anyone who sees someone in trouble and does nothing about it is not a true Muslim.

An ignorant person who is generous is nearer to Allah than a person full of prayer who is miserly. (Hadith)

The *intention* of the giver is important. A person must not give just to be noticed and admired by others.

DON'T CAUSE EMBARRASSMENT

People should not embarrass the needy.

Do not deprive your charitable deeds of all worth by...hurting [the feelings of the needy] as does he who spends his wealth only to be seen and praised by men but believes neither in Allah nor the Last Day.

(surah 2:264)

The only time for public giving is to encourage others to give.

THE RIGHT TO THE BASIC NECESSITIES OF LIFE

There are enough resources for everyone in the world. No human being should suffer need while others waste what they have. The hungry should be fed, the naked clothed and the wounded or sick should be given treatment. This applies to Muslims and others, whether they are friends or enemies.

Many Islamic charities organize help on a large scale. Some of the best known are listed below.

Islamic Relief
517 Moseley Rd
Birmingham B12
0121 440 3114

An international organization that helps needy Muslims in the UK and abroad

Muslim Aid
PO Box 3
London N7 8LR
0171 609 4425

Similar to Islamic Relief

The Red Crescent

Equivalent to the Red Cross

Muslim Women's Helpline
0181 908 6715
and 904 8193

Non-judgemental, caring support for Muslim women and girls

Helpline
0181 427 1751

Advice on anything, e.g. housing, racism; an offshoot of the paper *Muslim Voice*

Raising money for Islamic Relief

FOR DISCUSSION

'Giving publicly is not as worthy as giving privately.' When might this *not* be true?

FOR YOUR FOLDERS

1 What do you think the Prophet meant by the following Hadith:

How can you call yourself a believer while your brother goes hungry?

2 Explain the difference between zakah and sadaqah.

3 Why do Muslims believe a generous but ignorant person is better in the eyes of God than a religious miser?

CAUSES OF CRIME

Muslims believe that the devil is responsible for the four main causes of crime:

- deprivation and poverty
- lack of moral awareness
- lack of belief in God and the afterlife
- temptation and the urge to sin.

THE NATURE OF PUNISHMENT

The five main reasons for punishment are:

- control – to remove the offender from society so that no more damage is done
- retribution – to satisfy the need to see the offender get the punishment they deserve
- reform – to change the offender's ways
- rehabilitation – to help the offender start a useful new life in society
- reconciliation – society can receive back and forgive the offender.

JUSTICE – HUMAN, MUSLIM AND DIVINE

Muslims believe in strict justice, tempered with mercy. If people do wrong things and this is ignored, then it puts other people in the wrong. They have allowed an evil person to 'get away with it'.

Punishment removes the offender from society

If a person does wrong to themselves in private, then it is between them and God. If they do wrong in public, or boast of it, then they may have to be punished for the good of society.

The *victims* of crime must have their right to justice satisfied first, before a wrongdoer can be forgiven. The victim can forgive, ask for compensation or insist on punishment. The victim should reason with the offender and hope they will stop offending and become a friend.

NO ONE IS ABOVE THE LAW, OR UNPROTECTED BY IT

No one is ever above the law, no matter how powerful. Every one is protected by the law, no matter how humble.

No one should ever be sent to prison unless they have been convicted of a crime by a court of law that is properly set up.

PUBLIC JUSTICE

Muslims believe that justice should be carried out in public because:

- justice must be seen to be done
- judges or police should not have the opportunity for corrupt or brutal behaviour behind the scenes.

Muslims strongly disapprove of trials and punishments being carried out in secret, with the risk of inhumane treatment and torture.

PUNISHMENTS

Some harsh punishments are laid down by Islam and may be carried out in the stricter countries. These are generally for offences such as theft or murder. People can be flogged for drinking alcohol.

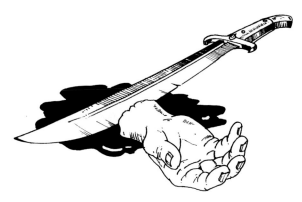

'As to the thief…cut off their hands: a punishment by way of an example' (surah 5:41)

THEFT

> A woman…was brought to the Prophet accused of theft, and they begged that she be spared the punishment. He said, 'I swear…that even if my daughter Fatimah had committed this crime, I would have amputated her hand myself.'
>
> (Hadith)

Although the Qur'an lays down a severe punishment for theft (cutting off the hand), a true Muslim would not steal, mainly because of the belief that Allah sees everything.

However, if a theft has happened, all the circumstances leading up to the offence are taken into account. If the person stole to feed the family and the State was not providing for them, then there would be no question of losing a hand. Hands are only amputated when it can be shown that the thief will not reform.

Muslim teachers sometimes show that Isa's saying on the subject ('*If thy hand offend thee, cut it off! It is better to go through life maimed than with both hands to enter hell,*' Mark 9:43) is supported by the Qur'an.

What may seem barbaric in the West is a point of honour for Muslims. Justice is applied equally to all with no exceptions.

FINAL JUDGEMENT BEFORE ALLAH

> Let them bear, on the Day of Judgement, their own burden in full – and also [something] of the burdens of those without knowledge whom they misled!
>
> (surah 16:25)

Muslims believe that human decisions can be wrong. They may be influenced by bias or ignorance of the circumstances. But Allah sees and hears everything, so no one can escape His judgement on their life. On that Day no one will be able to make excuses for another. Everyone will stand alone.

TALKING POINT

Citizens in the West insist that Muslims living in their countries should obey the laws of the land. Should they accept the same principle when they live in Muslim countries, and accept Islamic law?

FOR YOUR FOLDERS

1 What punishment does the Qur'an set for theft?

2 Why would a true Muslim choose not to steal?

3 What circumstances should a Muslim court take into account before cutting off a hand?

4 Why do Muslims believe that punishments should be carried out in public?

5 What does surah 16:25 teach about those who may seem to have escaped punishment in this life?

Jihad, or 'striving' comes from a word that means effort. In particular, it is any effort made by someone out of love for Allah.

THE GREAT JIHAD

For most Muslims, jihad is a personal effort that everyone makes to serve Allah to the best of their ability. They do this by living a life devoted to God, by self-sacrifice and by showing love and compassion (kindness) to others.

It is jihad when a Muslim:

● makes a special effort, e.g. getting up before sunrise in order to pray

● tries to love and forgive someone who has hurt or insulted them

● gives up personal possessions for the benefit of other people.

PEACE

Wars are wasteful of life and resources. Millions of people, including whole generations of soldiers and civilians, have died because of war. Billions of pounds are spent on warfare. No one could believe it is right to inflict suffering in order to take power or land by force. When this happens, Muslims regard it as tyranny. Tyranny is the cruel and oppressive rule of a country. Someone who rules in this way is a tyrant.

When a tyrant rules there is no real peace because:

● there is no security

● people feel humiliated and ashamed if they allow the situation to continue

● people feel helpless because they cannot do anything about it

● people feel ashamed because they think they have behaved in a cowardly way.

If anyone walks with an oppressor to strengthen him, knowing that he is an oppressor, he has gone forth from Islam.

(Hadith)

DEFENDING HONOUR AND JUSTICE

Islam is meant to be a religion of peace and goodwill. But Muslims do not agree with wrongdoing, and may fight to the death in defence of honour and justice.

Muslims feel obliged to fight against injustice and evil, and to show courage, obedience and discipline as they try to bring about a just and righteous society.

However, Muslims feel they should always exercise self-control and only fight for a principle, and not out of passion.

MILITARY JIHAD

The Prophet was asked about people fighting [for various reasons]: which of them fights for the cause of Allah? He replied, 'The person who struggles so that Allah's word is supreme is the one serving Allah's cause.'

(Hadith)

The word 'jihad' is often used in connection with a military conflict. Jihad does not mean forcing others to accept Islamic beliefs. It means striving to bring about a just society where Muslims can follow Allah's laws, and others can worship God or not, as they choose.

Holy War (Harb al-Muqadis) can follow on from jihad, but should only be declared:

● in *defence* of the cause of Allah, not for conquest

● to restore peace and freedom of worship

● to gain freedom from tyranny

● if led by a spiritual leader and fought until the enemy surrenders.

Kurdish guerilla fighters

Women, children and old or sick people should not be harmed, and trees and crops should not be damaged.

Jihad does not include:

- wars of aggression or ambition
- border disputes or national or tribal conflicts
- the intent to take over another country
- forcing people into accepting a faith they do not believe.

HUMANE TREATMENT OF ENEMIES

Muslims believe that a military jihad should stop as soon as the tyrant has surrendered. Once the enemy is beaten, all fighting should stop and the principle of mercy should apply immediately. The enemy should never be executed as revenge after they have surrendered.

The wounded of the enemy's army should receive the same treatment as one's own wounded. Women and children should never be harmed or ill-treated.

> If two sides among the believers quarrel, make peace between them. But if one trespasses…against the other, then fight against the one that transgresses until it complies with the command of God… then make peace between them with justice, and be fair, for God loves those who are fair.

(surah 49:9)

MARTYRS

A person who dies serving Allah is called *shahid*, a martyr. Muslims believe that anyone who becomes a martyr will receive forgiveness for any wrongs they have committed during their lives, and they will go straight to Paradise.

THINKING POINT

Just because there is no actual war does not mean that a country is 'at peace'. What else is needed?

FOR YOUR FOLDERS

1 Explain the meaning of jihad, shahid and tyrant.

2 What is the true meaning of jihad?

3 Give some examples of jihad in the everyday life of a Muslim.

4 What are the rules for a military jihad?

Islam is a worldwide religion with believers of every nationality

MULTI-RACIAL ISLAM

Islam teaches that loyalty to Allah is the only true loyalty, and this cuts across all barriers of race, colour and class.

Islam began in Arabia, near the starting places of Judaism and Christianity. Like these two faiths, it is now a worldwide religion with believers of every nationality.

The Prophet rejected nationalism.

> Nationalism means helping your people in unjust causes.
>
> (Hadith)

PREJUDICE

Some people are racist. They dislike people who are of a different race than themselves, or who have a different culture or religion. Many white people claim that black or brown people are not equal to whites. They may not like to see people wearing different clothes.

In the UK laws protect people from racial harassment, but not from religious harassment. A white Muslim would not be protected by the race laws.

HIJAB AND BEARDS

Issues like hijab (see unit 43) and beards for Muslim school pupils are difficult. This is because they are not compulsory according to the Qur'an – and millions of Muslims do not wear beards or hijab. They are sunnah (the example of the Prophet).

Most schools are sympathetic and allow girls to cover their heads and legs, as long as their clothing is neat and safe.

However, the *Muslim News* of 22 October 1993 reported that a head teacher in a school in Crawley, West Sussex, insisted on a Muslim boy shaving his beard and a girl removing her hijab. The Muslim community felt this was a clear case of discrimination against Muslims. Sikh boys *were* allowed to wear beards and turbans. The argument was that the issue was much more clear-cut for Sikhs than for Muslims. Massoud Shadjareh, spokesman for Muslims in Britain, complained that Sikhs and Jews were protected by the Race Relations Act 1976, but Muslims were not.

NATIONALISM

RACISM IN SOCIETY

Ibrahim Hewitt is a white Muslim. At a public meeting on *Racism, its effects on society*, he said that he had been laughed at, shouted at and sneered at while wearing clothes that showed he was a Muslim. He believes that racism is about religion, and not just the colour of a person's skin. 'Muslims are not a race,' he said, 'yet we suffer from racism.'

Other speakers at the meeting had different views. Moeen Yaseen, adviser for Muslim Schools, said that poverty, unemployment, homelessness and other things contributed to racial violence, and not just colour.

Dr Cyriac Maprayil of Tower Hamlets Race Equality Council agreed, but said that the majority of people being attacked in Tower Hamlets were Muslims. However, he disagreed that Muslims were 'doubly disadvantaged' (attacked for both their race and their religion). He said, 'When black people are attacked, they are not being attacked because they are Christians or Muslims.' A police spokesman reported that racist attackers were 'white, working class'.

(from a report in *Muslim News*, 29 April 1994)

HISTORICAL HANG-UPS

Some people still regard Muslims as 'the enemy' because of the Crusades of the Middle Ages. Some resent the fact that the Muslims won. History shows that the Christian Crusaders committed many bloody murders, while the Muslims were more moderate. But surely, these wars were long ago and it is time for reconciliation.

RELIGIOUS HANG-UPS

Others resent Muslims because they do not worship Jesus as the Son of God. But Muslims do *respect* Isa as one of the greatest people who ever lived, a miracle-worker and virgin-born prophet (see unit 17).

English and Malaysian Muslims praying together

FOR DISCUSSION

Some people are prejudiced against Islam because of reports of terrorists, antisocial behaviour, noisy political rallies and so on. It is unfair to judge Islam by these examples.

THINGS TO DO

1 Imagine you are a Muslim who has recently arrived in Britain. You may not understand the language and your skin is probably not white. How might racism affect your chances of feeling 'at home' in your new country?

2 Find out more about racism (using a dictionary or CD-ROMs). Collect press cuttings illustrating this problem and stick them on card to make a collage. Make an eye-catching logo, with a title such as 'Kick Racism Out'.

3 Why do you think Muhammad was so against nationalism?

Governing one's temper

> You shall not enter Paradise until you have faith and you cannot have faith until you love one another. Have compassion on those who you can see, and He Whom you cannot see will have compassion on you.

> (Hadith)

It takes a great deal of self-control to live life completely as a Muslim. Muslim beliefs in God and their constant awareness of His presence can help them to exercise the self-discipline they need.

ANGER AND BITTERNESS

The Prophet said:

> Allah holds back His punishment from him who holds back his anger.

> (Hadith)

Muslims are expected to have self-control in governing their temper and to make allowances for others.

It is right to get angry about things such as cruelty, tyranny, corruption and waste. This is righteous anger. But people should not react to ordinary irritations. The Prophet taught methods for dealing with anger – sit down if you are standing, or even lie down. He said that a soft word often turns away anger. Similarly, if people have been hurt they should not be bitter. Bitterness can spoil a person's life.

> Truly, anger spoils faith just as bitter aloes spoil honey!

> (Hadith)

> Bitter aloes – a sour drug made from herbs.

PRIDE

Arrogance and pride, acting as if you are superior, treating others as if they are inferior, being loud and boastful – all these are against the spirit of Islam.

> God does not love the proud or boastful. Be modest in your walk, and lower your voice, for the harshest of sounds is the voice of the ass!

> (surah 31:19)

This is not saying that God does not like donkeys! They are patient and helpful workers. This verse refers to the kind of people who bray about their achievements and successes.

ENVY

Muslims believe people should live in co-operation with others, not think of life as a competition. They should be helpful to everyone, whatever their race, colour, faith, culture or status.

Even people who tend to be quite prejudiced can control this against most groups, but the last (status) is hard. They become envious of other people's wealth, possessions, jobs, homes, cars or social position. The Prophet never used the phrase 'keeping up with the Joneses', but he did say:

> When you see someone who is wealthier than you, take a look at one who is less fortunate. ...Do not hold in contempt the favours Allah has shown towards you.

> (Hadith)

GREED

Muslims believe that they should not be too concerned about material things. Certainly they should not be greedy for more and more money and possessions. Gluttony is a form of greed – greed for food. The Prophet was against all forms of greed. Some people have a passion for collecting medals, trophies, sports awards. This is wrong, too. It is right to feel a sense of humble pride and satisfaction in doing something well. This is being thankful to God for his gifts. But greed usually involves grabbing and hoarding, and preventing others from sharing and enjoying.

BACK-BITING AND SUSPICION

No one likes people who talk about them behind their backs, either by saying nasty things about them or actually trying to bring them down. We may call this 'stabbing people in the back'. Most of us would prefer people to speak to our faces and give us the chance to defend ourselves from slander. In Islam, this is a command of Allah.

> O believers! Avoid suspicion, for suspicion is a sin. And do not spy on one another or backbite each other.
>
> (surah 49:12)

AGGRESSION

> God will not show mercy to the one who does not show mercy to others.
>
> (Hadith)

Islam teaches that Allah will not tolerate abuse and cruelty to any of His creatures. Muslims believe they should not be aggressive to people, or try to overpower them, physically or mentally, or be hurtful to their thoughts and feelings. Bosses should not make their workers feel small. Husbands and wives should not bully their partners by aggressive behaviour, or complaining, continual criticism or constant nagging.

Revenge and blood feuds are serious sins. Although equal retaliation is considered to be just, forgiveness is better.

FOR DISCUSSION

- Goodness and evil cannot be equal. Repay evil with what is better, and then the one who was your enemy will become your intimate friend.

  (surah 41:34)

- Beware of envy, for it eats up goodness as fire eats up fuel.

  (Hadith)

FOR YOUR FOLDERS

1 What is 'righteous anger'?

2 How does other anger spoil human life?

3 Why are pride and envy not part of the spirit of Islam?

4 How can a person deal with feelings of pride and envy?

5 In what ways could it be said that a person's worst enemy is him- or herself.

No one trusts a liar

Dishonesty comes in many forms, and Muslims believe Allah (Who sees everything) asks them to steer clear of all of them.

LYING

No one trusts a liar. Once a person has been caught out in a lie, no one can ever be really sure they will not do it again. No one really trusts a liar.

The Prophet said that even if a person prayed and fasted, that would count for nothing because of his lies.

> If you do not give up telling lies, God will have no need for you giving up food and drink [in fasting].
>
> (Hadith)

SLANDER

Some people lie to get themselves out of trouble. It is worse when they lie to hurt others or get them into trouble.

Slander (spoken accusations and lies against others) and libel (written lies) are particularly hard to deal with. The slandered person cannot fight back and put the record straight. Rich people can go to court, but ordinary people cannot afford to do this. Even when you have cleared your name it is difficult to wipe the slate clean.

The Prophet's young and beautiful wife Aishah was once accused of adultery. She could not prove her innocence, and was helpless to stop the things that people were saying and thinking about her. Then Allah gave the Prophet a special revelation.

> Those who love to spread slander about the believers will have a painful punishment in this world and the next!
>
> (surah 24:14)

FRAUD

Fraud is forbidden to Muslims, whether on application forms, tax returns or in business.

CHEATING

The Prophet was greatly admired for his honesty when he was a trader. He particularly despised cheats, and delighted in people who had the opportunity to cheat but did not do so.

> On the Day of Resurrection Allah will not look at…the person who swears [to the truth] while lying about his merchandise.
>
> (Hadith)

Muslims believe that it is foolish to sell your hopes of Paradise for the things of this world (see unit 20).

> The truthful and trustworthy merchant is associated with the prophets, the upright and the martyrs.
>
> (Hadith)

ABUSE

Foul language, obscenity and unpleasant name-calling are forbidden to Muslims.

GAMBLING

Although some people regard gambling as harmless fun, Muslims do not. They believe that Allah discourages it because some people become addicted and it has a bad effect on their family, finances and character. Muslims believe people should work for what they want in life.

> Humans shall have nothing but what they have struggled for.
>
> (surah 53:39)

DIVINATION AND KUFR (UNBELIEF)

Kufr is when people stop trusting God. They may try to gain hidden knowledge or power over others through 'spirit forces' or suchlike. Divination is the attempt to predict the future by horoscopes, astrology, crystal balls, magic or mediums. The Prophet counted magic as one of the deadly sins.

> Avoid the seven destroyers…shirk, magic, unlawful killing, usury, taking the property of orphans, fleeing from the battlefield, and slandering virtuous women who are indiscreet.
>
> (Hadith)

At the time of the Prophet there were many soothsayers and diviners. These people claimed to be able to see into the future through contact with jinn (beings from the spirit world) – rather like psychics with crystal balls or ouija boards.

Some people use them for cursing others and wishing evil on them. The Prophet warned:

> Whoever curses a thing…the curse will rebound upon the curser.
>
> (Hadith)

The Qur'an makes it clear that divination is false and misleading.

> No one in the heavens and the earth knows the Unseen except Allah.
>
> (surah 27:65)

It is haram to consult mediums about the secrets of the universe, or to ask for help from people who offer magic cures for illness or infertility or to remove difficulties.

Muslims do not believe in carrying charms or reciting incantations (good luck spells). They do not agree with wearing little Qur'ans on chains, or lockets containing verses. Muhammad once saw a man wearing a brass bracelet and asked what it was for. The man said it was to protect him from weakness. The Prophet said:

> This only increases your weakness. Throw it away, for if you die wearing it, you will never achieve success.
>
> (Hadith)

FOR DISCUSSION

- Gambling, astrology and lucky charms are just harmless fun.
- It is OK to lie if it avoids upsetting people.
- Raffles and lotteries to raise money for good causes are not really gambling.

FOR YOUR FOLDERS

1 Make a list of the ways in which lying, cheating, gambling and divination could hurt others.

2 How far is it possible to forgive the person who lies or cheats and forget the hurts they caused?

3 Muslims think that lying, cheating and using magic show lack of trust in God (kufr). Do you agree? Explain your answer.

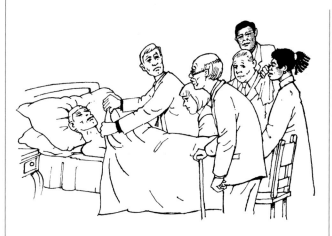

Death is not the end of everything

DEATH

Muslims believe that every life has its own set length and no one knows when their life will end. Therefore it is the duty of all Muslims to live every day as though it might be their last. Then they can be ready to face Allah and answer to Him for the way they have lived.

> The knowledge of [the final hour] is with my Lord, none but He can reveal when it will occur… All of a sudden it will come to you.
>
> (surah 7:187)

Some people pray to put off their death, asking for a miracle that will keep them alive. Others long to die because they are in great pain.

> When their time expires, they will not be able to delay it for a single hour, just as they cannot bring it forward [by a single hour].
>
> (surah 16:61)

No true Muslim should fear death as Muslims believe in the afterlife. Death is not the end of everything, and this should be a time of joy and reward for all their efforts on earth.

SUICIDE

Muslims believe that every soul was created by Allah and belongs to Him. This means that no person owns their own soul. For Muslims to kill themselves is as bad as killing other people unlawfully.

Life may be difficult, but Muslims believe that hardship is sent as a test that they should face with patience and humility. People should never be so full of despair that they commit suicide. However, many suicides happen as a result of mental illness or when the 'balance of mind is disturbed'. In these cases the people are not responsible for their actions.

EUTHANASIA

Euthanasia is sometimes called mercy killing. It can bring a gentle and easy death. People may think this is a kind thing to do when someone is in great pain or suffering.

Muslims reject this idea. They believe that Allah knows when people suffer. Besides, mercy killing does not always give the affected person any choice in the matter.

Muslims believe that the soul is perfect, even though the body that houses it may be damaged. Allah knows the reasons for our sufferings and the tests that come to us.

This may seem unfair at the time, but Muslims believe that Allah will reveal everything in time, and that Allah is always just.

CAPITAL PUNISHMENT

> Do not take life except for just cause. If anyone is wrongfully killed, We have given his heir the right [to demand retribution or to forgive]…
>
> (surah 17:33)

In Islam the two crimes that are just cause for giving the death penalty are:

- murder
- someone who has previously been a believing Muslim openly attacking Islam.

The Prophet supported the justice of taking a life for a life, but only through a proper court of law and a trial.

One of Muhammad's sayings suggests that the death penalty could be given for an ex-Muslim attacking Islam. Muslims are not condemned to death simply for leaving the faith.

ABORTION

> Slay not your children…the killing of them is a great sin.

(surah 17:31)

Abortion is only lawful in Islam when the life of the mother is at stake. Muslims believe the life of the mother is more important than that of the foetus (unborn baby) as she has responsibilities. She is actually alive, while the foetus has not yet formed a personality.

Some women insist they have the right to choose whether to give birth to a child.

Abortion is only lawful if the life of the mother is at stake

Muslims argue that this ignores the fact that another life is involved – the child's. The Qur'an reminds parents that on Judgement Day the infants will want to know why they were killed (surah 81:7–9).

Some Muslim scholars believe that the soul does not enter the body until the end of the fourth month of pregnancy and therefore abortion in the early days is allowed. Others say that no one really knows the answer to this question except Allah. Therefore the foetus is a potential human life from the moment of conception, and should receive all the protection and rights of all human life.

FOR YOUR FOLDERS

1 Good Muslims live with a constant awareness of death. Is it a bad thing to think about death like this? Explain your answer.

2 Why should good Muslims live every day as if it were their last?

3 Explain the meaning of suicide, euthanasia and abortion.

4 Why are suicide and euthanasia regarded as crimes in Islam?

5 When is abortion allowed in Islam?

FOR DISCUSSION

If Allah fixes human life spans, how might this influence a person's attitude to war, illness and disaster?

HUMAN NEEDS

In addition to spiritual and intellectual needs, people also have physical needs that must be satisfied. The sex drive is a normal part of human physical nature and Islam teaches that it should be satisfied in a wholesome and pure manner.

> When a husband and wife share intimacy it is rewarded...; just as they would be punished if they engaged in illicit sex.
>
> (Hadith)

Muslims do not believe that sex is unclean, or that it should be resisted or suppressed. On the other hand, they do not believe that people should take part in sexual pleasures without concern for morality. Sex without morals leads to an unhealthy preoccupation with sex, and even using sex as a business.

Muslims believe that these are two extremes that go against human nature. The ideal is that sexual desires must be satisfied, but the individual and the family must be kept from harm.

PERMISSIVENESS

Permissiveness is the view that people should set their own rules for living. Muslims believe that permissiveness leads to selfishness, rape, lying, drug addiction, theft and even murder. Muslims who listen to Allah should be able to resist temptation and know right from wrong.

SEX BEFORE MARRIAGE

> Let no man be in privacy with a woman who is not lawful unto him, or Shaytan will be the third.
>
> (Hadith)

Muslims do not believe that a couple having sexual freedom before they are married will add anything to the future of their relationship. In countries where sexual freedom is tolerated, the rate of divorce is high.

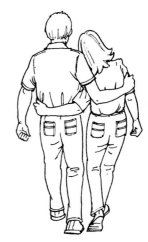

Courtship may not end in marriage

Muslims believe that someone who has had many previous sexual contacts may not prove to be a faithful partner in marriage.

The Prophet commanded that couples should meet and allow feelings of love, closeness and companionship to develop. However, they should always be *chaperoned*, which means that another adult should supervise their meeting.

COURTSHIP

Courtship does not always end in marriage, so a woman's chastity (purity) and reputation must be protected. A selfish man could take advantage of a girl for his own satisfaction, and then dump her, possibly even leaving her pregnant.

ADULTERY

A person having sexual relations with someone other than their husband or wife (adultery) undermines the security of the family. Most people find it impossible to forgive, as the feelings of hurt and betrayal are too great. They feel they can never trust their partner again.

Therefore Muslim men are forbidden to tempt married women, and a wife should never betray her husband's trust.

According to the Qur'an the penalty for adultery is flogging with 100 lashes. Sometimes an adulterer could be executed. The death penalty is not in the Qur'an, but some Muslims justify it from Hadiths.

Non-Muslims may think these penalties for adultery are severe. However, Muslims cannot understand why divorce is so difficult in Western countries. Muslims believe divorce should be quick, dignified and simple. Adultery shows lack of self-control and offends family honour.

> Have nothing to do with adultery, for it is a shameful thing…
>
> (surah 17:32)

> The man and woman guilty of adultery or fornication, flog each of them with a hundred stripes; do not be moved by pity.
>
> (surah 24:2–3)

HOMOSEXUALITY

Muslims do not regard homosexuality as a normal part of life. They consider that it is against the laws of nature.

Muslims think homosexuality is either a sickness or a depraved (bad) practice. They believe it happens when people are addicted to sex, when the opposite sex is not available to them, or when they fear or dislike the opposite sex.

> If two people are guilty of [unlawful sex], punish them both. If they repent and change [their ways] leave them alone… Allah accepts the repentance of those who do evil in ignorance and repent soon afterwards…
>
> (surah 4:16–18)

In Islam, the only form of sexual activity that is allowed is that which takes place within marriage. Therefore, on these grounds alone, homosexuality is unacceptable.

The Prophet said that neither sex should imitate the other in their way of speaking, walking, dressing or moving. This kind of behaviour represents conduct that goes against nature.

FOR DISCUSSION

- People in the Western world have become obsessed with sex.
- Many people would be more contented with life if sex was not seen in the media so much.
- Girls need protecting from sex-hungry men and boys.

FOR YOUR FOLDERS

1 Why do Muslims think it is best if sex only takes place within marriage?

2 What is the Muslim attitude to homosexuality?

3 Why do you think the penalties for sexual misconduct (adultery, homosexuality) are so severe in Islam?

Islam prohibits the abuse of drugs, alcohol and tobacco

Intoxicants are the key to all evils. A man was brought and asked either to tear the Holy Qur'an, or kill a child, or bow in worship to an idol, or drink a cup, or sleep with a woman. He thought the less sinful thing was to drink the cup, so he drank it. Then he slept with the woman, killed the child, tore the Holy Qur'an and bowed in worship to the idol.

(a story of Uthman bin Affan)

Muslims are forbidden to drink alcohol in any form. The reason is that alcohol causes people to lose control of their minds and bodies.

Muslims use the word *khamr*, which means intoxicant or poison, and explain it as 'anything that befogs the mind'.

ISLAMIC PROHIBITION

At the time of the Prophet many people drank a great deal of alcohol. The teachings in the Qur'an take human weakness into account, and the ban on alcohol was introduced in stages (surahs 16:67, 2:219).

Muslims were asked not to come to prayer with their minds fogged with alcohol (surah 4:43). As prayers were said five times a day, it meant that those obeying the order to pray were virtually giving up alcohol. Finally, the complete ban came (surah 5:93–4). When news of the latest revelation spread through Madinah, people poured away the drinks in their hands and smashed their wine containers, pouring the wine into the sand.

Muslims believe that alcohol is the devil's most successful trick to combat belief in Allah. It is a powerfully addictive drug. People often continue to drink even when they know it is doing them harm. They give someone a drink when they are shocked, bereaved or upset. The media show drinking alcohol as a pleasant social habit.

Alcohol is not a medicine but a disease.

(Hadith)

A Muslim would only be allowed alcohol if it was in a medicine and there was no alternative available.

KEEPING A BARRIER

True Muslims believe that even being in the presence of alcohol is a danger, and try to

TOBACCO

keep a barrier between themselves and any contact with drink. Some Muslims, however, have adapted to living in a society that accepts alcohol. They will sit with friends who drink, in pubs or at home, even though they themselves will have fruit juice.

Muslims are forbidden to:

- trade in alcohol
- own or work in a place that sells it
- sell grapes that they know will be used to make wine
- give alcohol as a present, even to a non-Muslim.

DRUGS

Drugs such as marijuana (hashish), cocaine, crack, smack and ecstasy are powerful intoxicants that affect the human mind and are therefore khamr.

> Sinful people smoke hashish because they find it produces rapture and delight, an effect similar to drunkenness…it produces dullness and lethargy…it disturbs the mind and temperament, excites sexual desire, and leads to shameless promiscuity.
>
> (Shaikh Ibn Taymiyyah)

People often use drugs to escape from the pains and hardships of their lives. They flee to a world of fantasy where they experience a feeling of well-being – a 'high'. These feelings are false, not real. They can be dangerous and are against the spirit of Islam.

DISASTROUS EFFECTS OF DRUGS

Muslims are against drugs mainly because they are forbidden in the Qur'an. Also they harm people's minds, their general health and their ability to work. Drug abuse can cause mental breakdown, despair, bankruptcy and suicide. Drugs can damage family life by causing neglect and cruelty.

Because of the damage to their bodies, which Muslims believe are the property of Allah, drugs are haram.

The penalty for taking drugs or alcohol in an Islamic country is flogging.

SMOKING

The Qur'an does not mention tobacco as it had not been discovered at that time. But, if Islamic principles are applied, smoking should be considered haram. There is now no doubt that smoking is harmful to health. Muslims believe that people should give up smoking – or better still, not start.

FOR YOUR FOLDERS

1 'Every intoxicant is khamr, and every khamr is haram' (Hadith). What do khamr and haram mean?

2 Muslims know that it is hard to give up harmful habits. Why do they think people should be made aware of the serious consequences of their habits?

3 What other people, apart from the drinkers, are affected by alcohol abuse? (Think about family members, work colleagues, road users.)

4 How might the barrier against alcohol affect a Muslim in the UK?

5 In some countries where tobacco is grown, the local people live in poverty while the landlords grow rich on this export crop. What do you think Muslims would think about this?

MODERATION

The Prophet taught that Muslims were to be an ummah, a worldwide family. They should take the 'middle way'. They should be neither too casual nor too extreme about any aspect of life or belief. He said:

> Allah…has defined certain limits, so do not go beyond them; He has prohibited certain things, so do not do them; and He has kept silent concerning other things out of mercy for you, and not because He forgot to mention them – so do not ask questions (or cause divisions) because of these matters.

(Hadith)

This means that nothing is forbidden in Islam except what Allah Himself prohibited. No human authority, no matter how learned or devout or powerful, has the right to prohibit things allowed by Allah or to judge people who are acting according to their consciences.

ZEALOTRY

The Prophet took a stern view of believers who were so 'holy' that they made other people feel inferior. He called them zealots (fanatics) and trouble-makers. The trouble with zealots is that they look down on people who do not agree with their extreme views.

The Prophet was well aware that it was only human nature that some people would be far more devoted to God than others were. However, he also knew that some people had the wrong motives for wishing to be thought holy. The sin of the zealot is *excess*.

> O believers! Do not make unlawful those good things which Allah has made lawful for you, and commit no excess. God loves not those given to excess.

(surah 5:90)

SHIRK

Muslims believe Christians commit excess in religious terms. Christians teach that Isa (Jesus) is part of the three-fold God (see unit 17).

> O People of the Book! Do not exceed the bounds in your religion, transgressing beyond the truth!

(surah 5:80)

In Islam it is wrong to make an idol of any human being, however worthy. It would be very wrong to idolise a pop-star or sportsperson.

EXTREMISM

The Prophet taught that people should not go to extremes in practising their religion. This only makes other people feel uncomfortable.

If a Muslim wishes to spend extra time praying and reciting the Qur'an, the Prophet said they should do it in private and in their own time. Public prayers should be fairly short, out of consideration for others. He once discovered that a friend avoided going to the mosque because the imam took too long and was over-zealous. He told off the imam!

A Muslim man might want to spend as much time as possible at the mosque. The Prophet

The qiblah of a mosque

said this was not right if it meant neglecting his wife and family. The Prophet said, '*Do not make your houses graves!*' (i.e. places where they could not pray).

Another example was when a very religious woman fasted so often that her husband could not have intimacy with her during the day (fasting includes no sex, see unit 31). The Prophet said she should only fast with his permission.

'Good points' earned for a Muslim's love of Allah can be cancelled out by 'bad points' earned for neglecting the rights of others.

FUNDAMENTALISM

Fundamentalist Muslims want to keep to the original teachings of Islam without accepting any later additions or new ideas. However, it is not always clear what the original teachings were, especially regarding some Hadiths.

Fundamentalism grew during the years when Muslim lands were under Western rule. Traditional Muslim education was set aside in favour of a Western system. This limited the number of scholars who could gain an advanced knowledge of Islam. If Muslims do not have enough background knowledge of Hadiths, they may pick up unsound teachings and express views that may be the very opposite of true Islam.

The more extreme fundamentalists may try to force their views on others. No person should ever try to force another to believe or do anything in Islam.

> The Truth stands out clear from error.
>
> (surah 2:256)

COVERING FAULTS

The real spirit of Islam is not always to be looking for error in others, but to cover faults – that is, to pass over them gently.

It is part of the mercy of Allah that you deal gently with people…so pass over [their faults] and ask for [God's] forgiveness for them.

(surah 3:159)

HYPOCRISY

Muslims believe they must practise what they preach. People have no respect for someone who talks about their strong beliefs but has a lifestyle that doesn't match up. This person is really living a lie, and this is called hypocrisy.

FOR DISCUSSION

- Muslims who are 'too holy' drive more people away from God than they bring to Him.

- Extremists care more about themselves than they do about God.

FOR YOUR FOLDERS

1 Explain the meaning of zealotry, extremism and fundamentalism.

2 Explain what is meant by:

   a hypocrisy   **b** 'covering' faults.

3 Imagine your mother or teacher tells you to do something but you make a mistake. How would you like them to behave towards you when they find out?

4 The Prophet said, 'Seek knowledge from the cradle to the grave,' (Hadith). How might better education help to avoid extremism and fundamentalism?

THE SUCCESSORS

For 30 years after the Prophet died, Muslims were ruled by four khalifahs. Khalifah means 'successor'. These were outstanding men who were chosen by the community for their closeness to the Prophet and their good characters. They had been the Prophet's closest friends and knew his ways and his attitudes.

WAY OF LIFE

Although they had access to enormous wealth, the khalifahs lived very simple lives, as the Prophet had done. They ate little and wore patched clothes. They refused to take anything for themselves that they did not actually need.

They were kind and just, and dedicated to serving the people. Although they were the most important people in the Muslim state, they refused to allow anyone to think of them as kings. They were servants. Only God was King.

RULES OF THE KHALIFAHS

- No khalifah would make a law contrary to the law of God. If he did, no one was to obey it.

- Justice was to be done and oppression was to be put down.

- There was to be food, shelter, education and care for everyone.

- Good was to be encouraged and evil was to be overcome.

ABU BAKR

Abu Bakr, the first khalifah, was the father of the Prophet's youngest wife, Aishah.

Many Muslims wanted the Prophet's son-in-law, Ali, as khalifah, but Abu Bakr was the senior Muslim and he was elected. Ali's wife, Fatimah, the Prophet's daughter, was very hurt, but Ali stood aside.

Abu Bakr was already 60 years old when he became khalifah and only ruled for two years, during 632–4 CE. He was called *As-Siddiq* ('witness to the truth') and *Amirul Muminin* ('ruler of the believers').

As he was dying, he nominated Umar as his successor. Ali and his supporters thought this was wrong, but again Ali accepted the situation.

SOME SAYINGS OF ABU BAKR

- O People, I have been chosen by you as your leader, although I am no better than any of you. If I do well, give me your support. If I do wrong, set me right!

- Always fear Allah; He knows what is in men's heart.

- Be kind to those who are under your care and treat them well.

- Improve your own conduct before asking others to improve theirs.

- Honour the envoy of the enemy.

UMAR

Umar was a bald, giant of a man who had been one of Muhammad's chief advisers. He was khalifah during 634–44 CE.

During his reign Muslim warriors captured Syria and Palestine. The Christian ruler of Jerusalem, Sophronius, said he would only surrender to Umar himself. So in 637 Umar set out for the city, wearing his shabby, patched cloak, with one camel and a servant. He and the servant took turns to ride.

They discovered the temple in Jerusalem was falling down and had become a rubbish dump. Umar began to clear the debris with his own hands, and people joined in. They worked until the 'holy rock' was uncovered.

They built a simple wooden mosque nearby, on the site of King Solomon's palace. This was said to be the spot from which the Prophet ascended to heaven on his Night Journey (see unit 6).

One day, Umar was visiting the burial place of Isa (Jesus), the most important Christian shrine in Jerusalem. Just then, the call to prayer sounded. Umar immediately hurried away to say his prayers, so the Christians were able to keep their shrine. Otherwise it would have become a mosque. This is the contract Umar made with the Christians of Jerusalem:

> …Their churches shall not be taken away, nor shall they be pulled down, nor shall any damage be done to them…They shall not be forced to give up their beliefs, nor shall they be persecuted for them. [This] shall hold good so long as they pay the tax for their defence…

The Dome of the Rock, Jerusalem

DEATH OF UMAR

In 644 CE Umar gave judgement against a Persian slave, Firuz. Firuz wanted revenge. He waited until the dawn prayers, then he stabbed Umar six times while he was kneeling. Umar died three days later, having appointed a six-man committee to elect his successor.

SOME SAYINGS OF UMAR

- Do not be misled by a person's reputation.
- Don't judge a person by his actions but by his truthfulness and wisdom.
- He who has no idea of evil can easily fall into its trap.
- Judge a man's intelligence by the questions he asks.
- Be grateful when you are shown your faults.

FOR YOUR FOLDERS

1 What do you think were the qualities a person needed to be chosen as a khalifah?

2 Choose three of the sayings of Abu Bakr and write them out as a scroll. What do these sayings tell you about the character of Abu Bakr?

3 How was Umar's character revealed by:

   a his clothes

   b the way he treated his servants

   c his sayings?

4 What did Umar's activities in Jerusalem show about Muslim attitudes to Christians?

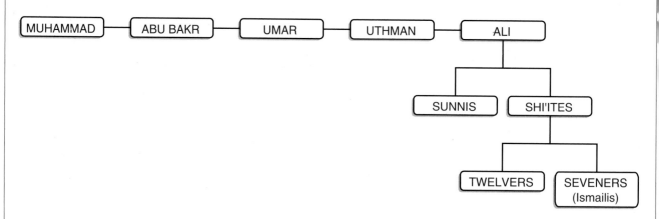

Divisions of early Islam

UTHMAN

After the death of Umar, Ali was invited to be khalifah on condition that he accepted the Qur'an, the sunnah and the recorded decisions of the previous khalifahs. Ali agreed to the first two but rejected the third. He had not agreed with some of these decisions at the time and would not agree to them now.

Then Uthman was invited to be khalifah on the same terms, and he agreed.

Uthman was a member of the **Ummayyad** family of the Quraish (see unit 1). He was the only one of his family to become a Muslim in the early days. He married two of the Prophet's daughters.

After his appointment he was rather weak in his discipline, and appointed members of his family and friends to key positions. Many people thought the Ummayyads were trying to take over and they resented this. Many Muslims tried to persuade him to retire when he was 80 years old, but he refused.

Then he replaced an Egyptian governor with one of his own family. Five hundred Egyptians came to reason with him, but he preached a public sermon against them. Later, when he was praying, a group of Egyptians killed him.

ALI AND HIS FAMILY

At last Ali was appointed khalifah, and he ruled during 656–61 CE.

There are many stories from Ali's young life.

One day he discovered the Prophet and his wife kneeling in prayer. He asked to whom were they prostrating themselves. The Prophet explained about Allah and the revelations he had received. Ali became so excited that he declared his belief the next morning. He was the first male convert to Islam.

When he was only ten, he attended a dinner when Muhammad was trying to persuade his family to believe. Ali stood up and said, 'I may be a boy…but O Muhammad, I shall be your helper. Whoever opposes you, I shall fight him as my mortal enemy.' The adults laughed, but Ali became known as *Asadullah* – 'the Lion of God'.

Ali married Fatimah, the youngest daughter of the Prophet. She had taken part in early Muslim battles and was highly respected. She and Ali had three children. Sadly she died at the age of 30, a few months after the Prophet's death. People said she was the perfect example of a woman, and her extended hand became a symbol for good fortune and divine protection.

OPPOSITION TO ALI

Uthman's cousin **Muawiya** opposed Ali's appointment. He was supported by the Prophet's surviving wife Aishah.

Ali had failed to track down or punish the killers of Uthman, because he understood their reasons for it. Muawiya and Aishah demanded that Uthman's murder be avenged.

In 656 CE Aishah fought Ali at the Battle of the Camel. She was taken captive and sent to Madinah. Ali moved to Kufa.

In 657 CE, at the Battle of Siffin, Ali overcame Muawiya, but agreed to joint discussions about his rule.

This caused great arguments among the Muslims, and ended with a split: Muawiya as khalifah in the North and West, and Ali as khalifah in the East. One group, later known as the Kharijites, were so angry with Ali's apparent weakness, they wanted to end the 'impurity' and conflict by killing both of them and starting again.

SOME SAYINGS OF ALI

- One who knows himself knows his creator.
- One who is proud of worldly possessions in this brief existence is ignorant.
- Learned men live after death; ignorant men are dead although alive.
- A sign of a stupid man is his frequent change of opinions.
- A hypocrite's tongue is clean, but there is sickness in his heart.
- Better alone than in bad company.

THE DEATH OF ALI

Ali half-expected to be assassinated but he refused to hide or run away. Ali was wounded while in the mosque at Kufa. While on his death-bed, Ali protected his attacker, and ordered that the man was to be spared if he survived, or killed quickly if he should die. The man's family was to be left alone.

Ali's last words were 'O God, *most fortunate am I!'*

QUICK QUIZ

1 Who was the third khalifah?
2 Which clan did he belong to?
3 Who was his cousin, who later opposed Ali?
4 What was Ali's nickname, and its meaning?
5 How did Uthman and Ali die?
6 What does the Hand of Fatimah symbolize?

FOR YOUR FOLDERS

1 Why did many Muslims resent Uthman as khalifah?
2 What led up to his assassination?
3 Why did the Kharijites oppose Ali?
4 What do the stories of Ali on these pages tell you about his character?
5 How was the kindness and courage of Ali revealed even while he was dying?

THINGS TO DO

Choose *four* of the sayings of Ali and write them out carefully, explaining in your own words what each one means.

THE SPLIT

The death of Ali created a crisis in Islam. Ali's supporters felt very strongly that it was Ali whom the Prophet had trained to be his successor, and he was, after all, the father of the Prophet's grandsons. They claimed that Abu Bakr had been elected while Ali was burying the Prophet. Those who supported Abu Bakr insisted *he* was the Prophet's choice and the senior Muslim at the time.

Now that Ali and Fatimah were dead, Ali's supporters insisted the next khalifah should be Ali's son, Hasan.

Muawiya, who had survived threats against his life, did not agree. In the end Hasan had an understanding that the khalifate would revert to Ali's family only after Muawiya's death. Hasan died (some said due to poison), and Muawiya named his own son **Yazid** as heir.

'ROYAL FAMILY' OR DEMOCRATIC LEADER?

The Muslims who supported the descendants of Muhammad became known as Shiat Ali or the Party of Ali. They are now called Shi'ites. They did not accept the first three khalifahs and said Ali was really the first, followed by the Prophet's grandsons, Hasan and Husayn.

Others claimed that only those who followed the Way of the Prophet, or sunnah, were true Muslims. They became known as the Sunni Muslims. About 90 per cent of all Muslims are Sunni. They believe in the Qur'an and Hadiths and the laws based upon them.

The Sunni insist that the Prophet intended that elections should take place to ensure that the *best* person would succeed. They say that it is wrong to claim there is a family line of rulers, like kings. The Shi'ite minority, about 10 per cent of Muslims today, are very devoted to their traditions, sometimes fanatically so. The number of Shi'ites is increasing as people in developing countries react against the moral failure of the modern world.

Shi'ism is now the state religion of Iran and is very strong in Pakistan, Iraq, India, the Yemen and the Lebanon.

THE MARTYRDOM OF HUSAYN

War broke out between Husayn and Yazid. In 681 CE, Husayn and his sister Zainab, with 70 supporters, were surrounded by Yazid's army at Karbala. They could not reach the river, and began to die of thirst.

Husayn had already foreseen his own death in a dream. He put on his grandfather's famous patched cloak and went out to face his enemies with his sister. He held out his baby son Abdullah, pleading for mercy for him. But an arrow pierced the baby's neck and pinned him to Husayn's arm.

Finally, Husayn was struck through by many arrows, and his head was cut off and taken to Damascus.

Eventually Yazid returned the head for burial. He also allowed safe passage for Zainab and Husayn's other son Ali Zain al Abidin who had been injured. Husayn's four-year-old grandson, Muhammad al Baqir, was also saved.

Husayn's shrine at Karbala became a holy place. Shi'ites hold a ten-day festival there every year to remember his martyrdom.

The main features of the festival are processions and passion plays, re-enacting Husayn's suffering. There are daily gatherings when people weep for the seeming triumph of tyranny over good.

They pledge themselves to keep up the fight to defend their faith and principles.

Sometimes the men in the processions gash themselves with knives and beat their backs with chains in memory of Husayn's wounds.

TWELVERS AND SEVENERS

Among the Shi'ites the title imam or leader of worship was used instead of khalifah.

The Shi'ites later divided into two main branches, according to whether they believed in seven or twelve imams. In each group, they claimed that the last of their imams mysteriously disappeared without dying. They believe that the Hidden Imam is unseen but still appears to the faithful in their times of need. He sends out his light to convert all humankind. He appears to people in prayer and gives the faithful strength in times of persecution. They believe he will eventually return to establish the rule of righteousness and bring about the end of the world.

Another name for the Hidden Imam is Mahdi. Some Shi'ites believe that the final Imam will be Isa (Jesus) returned to earth.

EXTREMISM

Shi'ites may be seen as fanatics because of their extreme devotion to their leaders. There are secret sects within Shi'ism. These attract people who are keen to protest against social injustice and against rulers who they think are corrupt. These members, who are often young, believe in violent protest and are prepared to die for their cause.

SHI'ITE ISLAMIC GOVERNMENT

Shi'ites and many Sunnis are dedicated to creating states where the government is based on the laws of Islam and the ruler is God alone.

QUICK QUIZ

1 What is a Sunni Muslim?

2 What is a Shi'ite Muslim?

3 What percentage of all Muslims are Sunni?

4 What are the two chief branches of Shi'ism?

5 What or who is the Mahdi?

6 Which countries have most Shi'ites?

7 Who was Husayn?

8 Where is Husayn buried?

FOR YOUR FOLDERS

1 Sunni Muslims often accuse the Shi'ites of paying too much respect to the family of Muhammad, and of 'adding' to Islam. Which beliefs are *added* by the Twelvers and Seveners?

2 Why do you think so many Shi'ite Muslims are prepared to be martyrs?

Shi'ite warriors for Allah

FIQH AND TASAWWUF

The Muslim religion has two parts – **fiqh** which has to do with the outward, observable part of worship, and **tasawwuf** which is concerned with the spiritual belief behind the actions.

Sufism is Islamic mysticism and is concerned with tasawwuf. Muslims apply both fiqh and tasawwuf to their worship. For example, in connection with salah, fiqh concerns:

- the correct washing (wudu)
- facing the correct qiblah
- the times for prayer
- the number of rak'ahs performed
- the correct way of performing the rak'ahs.

Tasawwuf concerns:

- the intention of the worshipper
- the depth of concentration
- awareness and love of God
- having a soul that is pure
- feelings of genuine communion with God
- the effect of prayer on morals and manners.

Sufism means being so open to God's presence that the believer feels drawn away from normal life. The believer seeks to be 'empty' of self and to pass from conscious thought to reach a state of union or oneness with God. The believer feels drawn to spend a great deal of time in prayer and contemplation. This is because the feeling of God's presence is so powerful that it is all the believer can think of. He may sometimes seem to be in a trance-like state. This kind of experience is the beginning of mysticism.

Sufis may belong to like-minded groups of people following a religious leader or **shaikh**. They can be Sunni or Shi'ite. They do not think of themselves as separate from other Muslims and usually worship in the same mosques.

MYSTICISM

It is difficult to explain what mysticism is. It is as if a person is lifted out of this world into another world where they may feel close to God. They are overcome by it, and feel so excited and thrilled that the rest of life becomes stale and of little importance by comparison. The mystic longs to experience this closeness with God again and again.

Sometimes it is a once-in-a-lifetime experience lasting only a few seconds or minutes. Some people develop methods to make it happen again. Others seem to have mystic experiences – without seeking them – throughout their lives.

AIMS AND GOALS

Sufis want to:

- give up the pursuit of wealth and luxury
- search for an inner, spiritual life
- experience communion with God
- become so close to God that their own identity is lost and absorbed into His
- give up all selfish appetites and physical desires.

LOVE

Sufism has produced many poets who tried to express their experience of the love of God – where God, self and love became mingled.

My heart is a pasture for gazelles…

Go sweep the chamber of your heart. Make it ready to be the dwelling-place of the Beloved. When you depart, He will enter it. In you, empty of yourself, He will display all His beauty.

(Shabistari)

TOLERANCE

My heart…is a pasture for gazelles and a monastery for Christian monks, and a temple for idols and the pilgrim's Ka'bah, and the tables of the Tawrah and the book of the Qur'an. I follow the religion of Love…

(Ibn Arabi)

Sufis are tolerant of other religions. They believe that God can be felt in many ways. The truth is what counts. Sufis tend to reject religious rules and regulations as 'aids for the unenlightened'. This view has caused orthodox Muslim leaders to be suspicious of Sufism.

The writings of the saintly woman **Rabia** reveal typical Sufi attitudes to the Ka'bah.

I see only bricks and a house of stone. It is only You, O God, that I desire.

(Rabia)

She is saying that the heart is the only true Ka'bah. Many orthodox Muslims would agree with this.

One great teacher, al-Hallaj, was crucified for claiming that he had become one with God. This was regarded as blasphemy – an insult to God.

TARIQAHS

The particular religious teachings about self that each group of mystics developed was called a **tariqah** ('way' or 'path'). Each Sufi group following a particular tariqah claims a chain of revelation that goes back to the Companions and the Prophet himself. Each has an inner circle of members known as **murids**. A murid is a disciple who is totally devoted to his or her shaikh or leader. A shaikh who is about to die usually chooses his successor, to whom loyalty is transferred.

Three tariqahs groups who claim descent from Ali (and are therefore Shi'ite) are the Qadiriyya, Chishtiyya and Suhrawardiyya. A group who claim descent from Abu Bakr are the Naqshbandiyya (see unit 75).

TALKING POINTS

1 Mystical experience is all in the mind – and a peculiar mind at that!

2 If religions are not ultimately all the same, then how can God truly exist?

FOR YOUR FOLDERS

1 Explain the meaning of fiqh, tasawwuf, tolerance, tariqah and shaikh.

2 How far is it true to say that 'love changes everything'?

3 How might a mystic experience change a person's life and way of thinking?

4 Why do Sufis think it is important to be 'emptied' of self?

5 Do you think that closeness to God is the most valuable experience there is? Give reasons for your answer.

THE IMPORTANT ROLE OF SUFISM

As Islam grew, many kings and rulers arose who were not true followers of the Way as set out by the Prophet. They were wealthy and powerful, but their spiritual qualities were poor. Their religious teachers concentrated on doing the right thing, but gave little importance to inner qualities.

Many people believe that Sufism saved Islam from becoming too concerned with following rules. Sufis concentrated on the love of God and the way of the Prophet. Their humility, sincerity and devotion had a great impact on those who met them.

Some oppressive rulers and power-hungry religious teachers persecuted the Sufis. They resented and feared their popularity. Sometimes the Sufis went 'underground' to protect their teachings.

The Sufis were great scholars and writers who inspired thousands. They kept Islam alive when it was being persecuted, by giving believers hope and faith. They still maintain their stand against love of money and rule-keeping.

AL-GHAZZALI

Orthodox Muslims thought that Sufis who claimed to have a close relationship with God might fall into the sin of shirk (see unit 12).

Al-Ghazzali (1058–1111 CE), one of the great scholars of Islam, reassured them that this was not the case. Sufism, he said, continued the history of mysticism that went back to the prophets. He saved Sufism and did much to protect Islam from becoming a formal religion that was all show. His teachings were so powerful he became known as 'the Proof of Islam'.

JALAL UD-DIN RUMI

One famous Sufi mystic, **Jalal ud-Din Rumi** (1207–73 CE), founded the group known as 'whirling dervishes' in Konya, Turkey. He began to have visions at the age of six.

For him, acceptance of God's will was the highest form of self-sacrifice and the greatest proof of love. Love was what mattered, not knowledge, greatness or striving. To experience love was like God's light shining into all the dark places of the Earth and making them one.

Rumi was joined by another mystic – his 'beloved guest' – for a time. When they parted Rumi knew great grief and loneliness.

No one knows who his beloved guest really was, but the experience enabled him to become aware of the soul's separation from the Beloved, who is God. Fellowship with God filled him with great joy, made him free from fear and carried him from loneliness to overwhelming love.

> God speaks to everyone…He speaks to the ears of the heart, but it is not every heart which hears Him. His voice is louder than the thunder, and His light is clearer than the sun – if only one could see and hear. In order to do that, one must remove this solid wall, this barrier – the Self.
>
> There are many roads to the Ka'bah…but lovers know that the true Holy Mosque is Union with God.
>
> (Rumi)

DERVISHES

Dervishes are members of brotherhoods or groups of Sufi **mystics**. The word dervish comes from a Persian word meaning 'beggar'. Another meaning is 'the sill of the door'. Some dervishes are wanderers and depend on alms to live. Some live in communities, others live as solitary hermits. They may practise particular exercises or **dhikrs** (see opposite) which bring them to the 'sill of the door', beyond which they believe is a holy light, or enlightenment.

The dance of the whirling dervishes

Dervishes believe that humanity is trapped in its own ignorance. They seek to be free from the world's cares and become channels for God's light. They reject 'empty' learning – knowledge for its own sake. They believe that personal experience is what counts.

A donkey may be loaded with books, but that does not make him intelligent.

You belong to the world of dimension, but you come from the world of non-dimension. Close the first shop and open the second.

(Rumi)

DHIKR

To 'open the second shop' requires devotion, will and a certain state of mind. The dhikrs are exercises to help this opening, and they include:

- intense concentration on God
- chanting religious phrases
- meditating on certain symbols
- breathing exercises
- the whirling dance, or **sama**, to bring about the loss of self and being taken up into God.

When the soul dances, every movement of life becomes a miracle.

(Rumi)

FEMALE MYSTICS

Sufis take it for granted that women also have mystical experiences. Two famous mystics were Rabia al-Adawiyya of Basrah (d.801 CE) and Sayyida **Nafisah** (d.824 CE) the great-grand-daughter of the Prophet's grandson Hasan. Both were famous for their learning and for their poetic expressions of love for Allah.

O God, if I have worshipped You for fear of hell, burn me in hell. If I have worshipped You for hope of Paradise, exclude me from it. But if I worship You for Your own sake then do not keep me from Your everlasting Beauty.

(Rabia)

FOR YOUR FOLDERS

1 Explain the meaning of persecution, dervish, dhikr and 'empty' learning.

2 Why do 'orthodox' Muslims and other Muslim leaders resent or even persecute Sufis?

3 Read carefully the mystical sayings of the Sufis in this unit. Choose two of them and try to explain what they mean.

FOR DISCUSSION

Attempting to expand mystical experience is dangerous and could be misleading.

The 'Naqsh' of the Naqshbandi order

ORDERS

There are three active Sufi orders, or groups, in Britain. These are the **Naqshbandis**, the Chishti and the Murabitun.

NAQSHBANDIS

The largest Sufi order worldwide is the Naqshbandi. It observes the shari'ah strictly and traces its origins back to Abu Bakr, the first khalifah. **Shaikh Nazim**, the current leader, is fortieth in this line.

He visits Britain every Ramadan and gives lectures at the Peckham mosque in south London. The mosque is a converted church and is run by the Turkish community. Every Ramadan it is host to Muslims from Britain, Germany, Malaya, America, Arabia and Spain. They come to learn more about spirituality and peace.

THE JOURNEY

When you go on a pilgrimage you need to find out where to go and how to get there. Then you think about what to take and what you need as regards food and baggage.

To the Sufi, Allah is the goal of the pilgrimage, the Shari'ah is the food and luggage, and the tariqah is the way. All tariqahs are ways that take people to the Divine Presence.

(Shaikh Nazim)

WHAT IS THE SUFI WAY?

Everyone has a destination or goal in their lives. Every prophet and religion has tried to show people how to reach their destinations. They brought laws which are 'outer ways' and 'inner ways'. Sufis teach that the inner way is the most important. When a person's inner life is right, then the outer life will be right, too.

Shaikh Nazim Adil al-Haqqani, khalifah of the Naqshbandi Sufis

Some people concentrate only on their outer life, but their inner life remains untouched. Humans are vain. Their ego (inner self) does not want to change, but always wants to take the easy route. Change takes effort. The goal of the Sufi Way is to change bad character into good character.

HEART

It is more important to conquer hearts than to conquer the whole world. When hearts are conquered, they come to surrender. Today we are in need of conquerers of hearts, and not doctors of Law.

(Shaikh Nazim)

LOSS OF SELF

When a person comes near to Allah, Allah's greatness makes him disappear. When you look at the sun, you are not able to see anything else.

(Shaikh Nazim)

DROPS AND OCEANS

As long as a drop is falling from the heavens it may be called a drop; but when it falls into the ocean it is no more a drop, it is an ocean.

(Shaikh Nazim)

MURABITUN

The leader of the Murabitun is a Scottish convert to Islam, Shaikh Abd-al-Qadir. He founded a Sufi community in London, then moved to Norwich in 1976. The Murabitun take their name from the Muslims who once ruled Spain and who used to build 'ribats' (fortresses) into which they retreated for study and spiritual training. The Murabitun ribats in the UK are not buildings, but are 'retreats into fellowship' of Sufi brothers and sisters as they strive for enlightenment. They are not separate from other Muslims, but meet at the local mosque.

THE CHISHTI

Members of the Chishti group seek inspiration through music. Chishtis feel that religious songs, called sama, can touch the soul in a special way. Only suitable music is allowed. Even religious music must be free from the desire to 'show off' or distract the believer from God.

Unlawful music includes:

- anything that stirs up immoral desires
- anything connected to lust or drunkenness
- anything habit-forming
- anything stirring up people for causes other than Allah, such as national songs.

FOR DISCUSSION

- Is it true that 'conquerors of hearts' are more important than 'doctors of Law'?

- What kinds of Western music would be unacceptable to the Chishti?

FOR YOUR FOLDERS

1 Write down the names of the three Sufi orders described in this unit. These groups have attracted many British Christians as converts. Why do you think this is?

2 Write a paragraph about each of the three Sufis mentioned in units 74 and 75 (Jalal ud-Din Rumi, Rabia and Shaikh Nazim).

There are many countries today where the majority of the population is Muslim. However, none of them is a perfect Islamic state based on Muhammad's Madinah.

Muslims share the hope that all citizens in an Islamic state would enjoy freedom of belief, thought, conscience and speech. They should be free to develop their full potential, both in their careers and their home lives. They should have the right to express themselves and support or oppose any government policy that they think is right or wrong.

An Islamic state would always follow the laws of the Qur'an and sunnah.

FEAR OF TERRORISM

When people hold very strong convictions, whether these are nationalist or religious, they may become involved in violence and unjustified, desperate actions. Many Muslims are prepared to kill or die for their beliefs.

Enthusiastic 'modernist' Muslims vehemently oppose:

- atheism (denial of God)
- not accepting the revelations of the Qur'an
- corruption
- private ownership of business
- love of money
- communism
- tyranny or oppression
- hypocrisy.

ATTITUDES TO MILITANT GROUPS

Politicians concerned with keeping the peace and building up their national economies may fear leaders of these groups. However, they are admired as heroes by poor people who:

- see the way corrupt politicians live in luxury

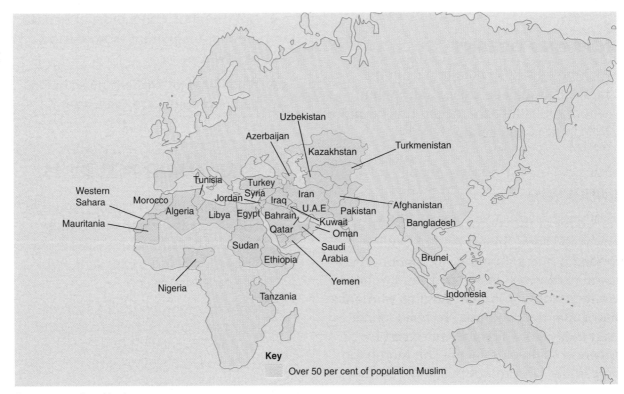

Key
Over 50 per cent of population Muslim

Countries with a Muslim majority

- do not themselves benefit from the wealth created by 'Muslim oil'
- feel they themselves are being made impure by alcohol, pornographic films, banks that charge interest, etc.

Less militant Muslims oppose these extreme movements. Some are happy to adapt to Western ways or to accept as much as seems good to them.

ISLAMIC REFORM

The desire for purity and spiritual renewal has led to Islamic reform movements in many countries in the Middle and Far East. They may be viewed as rebel or terrorist organizations.

The number of Muslims is growing rapidly. They make up over 80 per cent of the population of 32 countries, and over 50 per cent of 46 countries. Islam is now the fastest-growing religion in the UK and the USA. Millions are now able to say, 'I am Muslim and I belong to the Ummah'.

CONFLICT WITHIN ISLAM

There are groups in the Middle East with different aims that sometimes result in Muslim fighting Muslim. The key issues are:

- socialism – to improve the welfare of the people and to take religion out of politics
- Pan-Arabism – the desire for all Arabic-speaking peoples to unite (Pan means 'all')
- Pan-Islam – the desire for all Islamic peoples to unite.

Pan-Arabism aims to see a new empire of united states – a Union of Arabic Republics. However, although all Muslims learn Arabic for worship, not all are Arab. Pan-Arabism is about countries, whereas Pan-Islam is concerned with religion. Pan-Islam aims to bring about:

- true Islamic government under God
- a new rightly-guided khalifah (preferably a descendant of Muhammad)
- unity of Islam, especially Sunni and Shi'ite
- the reform of society
- the reform of Islamic higher education
- peace and justice for all
- freedom from tyranny (especially Western corruption, atheism and Zionism).

FOR DISCUSSION

- The most excellent jihad is to speak the truth in the face of a tyrannical ruler.

  (Hadith)

- Being wrong when you think you are right is the chief danger when you fight for your beliefs.

FOR YOUR FOLDERS

1 'Religion and politics are two separate things. Religious leaders should stay out of politics.' Do you agree? Give reasons for your answer.

2 Make a list of the chief aims of Pan-Islam and explain how it differs from Pan-Arabism.

3 Why do many political leaders regard Islam as a serious threat?

4 Islam approves of many aspects of socialism, but cannot accept communism. Can you explain why?

GLOSSARY

Abd servant or slave
Adhan the call to prayer
AH after the Hijra (Hegira)
Akhirah belief in life after death
Allah God
Allahu Akbar! 'God is great!'
Al-Qadr destiny, fate
Amal putting faith into action
Angel a messenger from God, usually invisible
Ansars citizens of Madinah who helped the Muslims
Aqiqah party for a new baby
Ayatollah a leading scholar in Iran

Baitullah House of Allah, the Ka'bah
Barzakh 'place of waiting' after death
Bedouin nomadic tribes of Arabia and North Africa
Bismillah 'In the name of God'

Calligraphy decorative writing
CE Common Era
Chador black cloak sometimes worn by Iranian women

Dhikr actions to bring on a mystic state
Din religious duty that affects a person's whole life
Du'a personal prayer or request to God

Fard obligations, things that *must* be done
Fatihah the first surah in the Qur'an
Fiqh outward, observable part of worship
Fundamentalist Muslims Muslims who want to hold on to the old ways of thinking

Ghusl bath taken for ritual cleansing

Hadith Qudsi sayings of God not found in the Qur'an
Hadiths sayings and traditions of Muhammad
Hafiz (plural **huffaz**) someone who can recite the Qur'an by heart
Hajj pilgrimage to Makkah
Halal allowed
Hanif a devout person
Haram forbidden
Hijab the veil worn by women in Islam
Hijrah the journey from Makkah to Madinah

Ibadah worship, being a servant of God
Iddah waiting time for divorce
Id-ul-Adha sacrifice-feast that ends the Hajj

Id-ul-Fitr feast at the end of Ramadan fast
Ihram state of religious 'separation' or purity
Ihsan realization of the existence of God
Ijma scholarly agreement to form a decision
Ijtihad using reason to decide correct action
Imam a teacher
Iman faith or belief
Immanent God's presence in the universe
Injil the Gospels, revelation to Isa (Jesus)
Iqra! Recite! – the command to Muhammad
Islam submission to God

Jahannam hell
Jamaah congregational (communal) prayer
Jihad personal striving for holiness, holy war
Jinn spirit or non-human entity
Jumu'ah Friday (day of Jamaah prayers)

Ka'bah the 'Cube', Holy Building in Makkah
Khalifah (1) deputy for God, successor
Khalifah (2) stewardship
Khitan circumcision
Khul divorce sought by wife
Khutbah sermon
Kiswah black cloth covering the Ka'bah
Kufr unbelief
Kursi small stool, stand for the Qur'an

Laylat-ul-Bara'at full moon before Ramadan
Laylat-ul-Mi'raj the Night of Muhammad's Ascent to Heaven
Laylat-ul-Qadr the Night of Power (when Muhammad received his first revelation)

Madrasah school
Mahr bride's dowry
Masjid Mosque, place of prostration
Mawlid an-Nabi birthday of Muhammad
Mihrab niche in Mosque showing the direction of Makkah
Minaret tower from which the call to prayer is given
Minbar pulpit for giving Friday sermons
Modernist Muslims Muslims who believe that the ideas of Islam need to keep up to date
Mosque place of prostration, for communal prayer and activities
Mu'adhin (**Muezzin**) the person who calls the faithful to prayer
Mubara'ah divorce by mutual consent
Muhajirun the Muslims who left Makkah

Muharram New Year
Mujtahid Shi'ite imam
Murid a Sufi initiate, one of the inner circle
Mystic someone who knows God through intuition or personal experience

Nabi a prophet
Nafs instinct to do good or evil
Nikah wedding ceremony
Niyyah intention

Purdah complete seclusion of women (they cover face and hands in public)

Qiblah the direction of Makah
Qiyam standing during prayer
Qiyas reasoning by analogy or comparison
Qur'an the Revealed Book of Islam
Quraish the leading tribe in Makkan region

Rak'ah the set movements in formal prayer
Ramadan the month of fasting
Rasul a prophet or messenger of God
Riba charging interest on loans of money
Risalah prophecy
Ruh the human soul
Ruku bowing during formal prayer

Sabr patience and fortitude
Sadaqah charity, voluntary giving
Sahifa the revelation given to Ibrahim (Abraham)
Salah ritual prayer, five times daily
Salam peace, also end of Salah prayer
Salat-ul-Janaza funeral prayers
Sama sacred dance used in Sufi rituals
Sawm fasting from sunrise to sunset
Shahadah declaration of faith
Shahid a martyr

Shaikh a tribal or spiritual leader
Shari'ah the way of life followed by Muslims
Shi'ite (Shiat Ali) Muslims who insist only a descendant of Muhammad can be khalifah
Shirk sin of comparing God to anything else
Subha string of prayer beads
Sufi a Muslim mystic
Sujud kneeling in prayer
Sunnah the way or example set by the Prophet
Sunni Muslim who follows the orthodox way
Surah a chapter in the Qur'an

Taharah purity, cleanliness
Tahnik part of naming ceremony
Takbir shutting out distraction before prayer
Talaq divorce procedure
Talbiyah Hajj prayer
Taqwa consciousness or awareness of God
Tariqah the Sufi way or path
Tasawwuf spirituality
Tawaf circling Ka'bah seven times on Hajj
Tawhid the teaching that God is one
Tawrah revelation given to Musa (Moses)
Tayammum symbolic washing without water
Tughyan arrogance, taking power for oneself

Ulama scholars
Ummah the 'family' of Islam
Umm-ul-Kitab 'mother of books', the Qur'an

Walima a feast or wedding party
Wudu ritual washing before prayer
Wuquf time of 'standing before God' on Hajj

Zabur revelation given to Dawud (David)
Zakah giving one-fortieth of savings for God's service
Zakat-ul-Fitr special charity gift in Ramadan

PLACES

Al-Badr site of Muhammad's first battle against the Makkans

Arafat Mount of Mercy where Adam and Eve met after God forgave them

Madinah (Madinat an-Nabi) the city of the Prophet, formerly Yathrib

Makkah birthplace of Muhammad, city of the Ka'bah shrine

Maqam Ibrahim place where Ibrahim prayed beside the Ka'bah

Mina place of stoning the Devil on Hajj Mount Nur (Mount Hira) Hill of Light, where Muhammad received his first revelation

Mount Nur (Mount Hira) Hill of Light, where Muhammad had his vision

Mount Thawr where Muhammad sheltered in a cave during Hijrah

Mount Uhud site of second battle against Makkans

Muzdalifah where pilgrims on Hajj camp, and collect pebbles to stone the Devil

Safa and **Marwah** places where Hajar searched for water

Taif mountain oasis where Muhammad was rejected

Zamzam well by Ka'bah revealed to Hajar

PEOPLE

Abd-al-Muttalib Muhammad's grandfather

Abdullah Muhammad's father

Abu Bakr friend of Muhammad, first khalifah

Abu Lahab Muhammad's uncle who opposed him

Abu Talib uncle who adopted Muhammad

Adam the first created man

Aishah youngest wife of Muhammad, daughter of Abu Bakr

Al-Ghazzali famous Sufi mystic

Ali son of Abu Talib, adopted by Muhammad; fourth Khalifah

Aminah Muhammad's mother

Azra'il the angel of death

Bilal Ethiopian slave, first caller to prayer

Dawud David, king of Israel

Eve first created woman

Fatimah one of Muhammad's daughters, married Ali

Hafsah Umar's daughter, one of Muhammad's wives

Hajar Hagar, second wife of Ibrahim

Halimah Muhammad's Bedouin foster mother

Husayn (Hussein) grandson of Muhammad

Iblis the devil, Shaytan or Satan

Ibrahim Abraham, 'father' of Jews and Arabs

Isa the prophet Jesus, worshipped by Christians

Isma'il the prophet Ishmael, son of Ibrahim

Israfil angel who takes souls to judgement

Jalal ud-Din Rumi famous Sufi mystic

Jibril (Gabriel) angel who brought revelations to Muhammad

Khadijah first wife of Muhammad

Maryam the Virgin Mary, mother of Jesus

Mika'il angel that protects the faithful

Muawiya the fifth khalifah

Muhammad the prophet chosen by Allah to deliver his message

Musa the prophet Moses

Nafisah famous Sufi woman mystic

Naqshbandis largest Sufi sect

Nuh the prophet Noah

Rabia famous Sufi woman mystic

Shaikh Nazim Sufi mystic

Shaytan Satan, the devil, the chief Jinn

Suleiman Solomon, son of Dawud (David)

Umar Muhammad's friend, second khalifah

Ummayyads a leading family in Makkah

Uthman Muhammad's friend, third khalifah

Waraqa ibn Nufal Christian cousin of Khadijah

Yazid son of khalifah Muawiya

Zaid ibn Haritha Muhammad's adopted son

Zaid ibn Thabit Muhammad's secretary, who compiled the written Qur'an

INDEX